BOOK 2 TWO

JOHN THOMPSON'S
ADULT PIANO COURSE

ISBN 978-1-4803-5312-1

Exclusively Distributed By

WILLIS MUSIC

HAL•LEONARD®
CORPORATION
7777 W. BLUEMOUND RD. P.O. BOX 13819
MILWAUKEE, WISCONSIN 53213

Visit Hal Leonard Online at
www.halleonard.com

CONTENTS

F O R E W O R D

The second book of *John Thompson's Adult Piano Course* continues the steady progression of what the student learned in Book 1. Concepts previously introduced will be reviewed in greater detail.

To compile a course of piano study for students who will never be seen, much less heard, is anything but an easy task. The difficulties are greatly increased when outlining a course for an adult student, since the word "adult" applies to teenagers as well as older beginners and grownups.

However, whether one is 6 or 60 years of age, the progressive points of pianism and musicianship remain the same. The only difference lies in the manner of presentation. And here is where the teacher becomes vitally important. They must be governed by the following:

1. The student's natural talent.
2. The mental capacity of each student.
3. Whether the student wishes to study seriously, including the theory and technique development necessary for expert pianism, or whether the desire is simply to "play for pleasure" avoiding tasks that might, from the student's viewpoint, be considered "work."
4. How much time the student is able and willing to devote to study.

The variables that result from the above must be met by a wise choice of supplementary material assigned to meet individual needs. For that reason, the Adult Course is elastic, presenting the various steps along the road in the most tuneful and palatable manner possible as to capture and hold the interest of those who are just taking piano "for fun," while at the same time laying a definite foundation for those who wish to pursue the study of piano seriously. (Be sure also to peruse Book 1 and 2 of the new *Popular Piano Solos* that were compiled and arranged specifically with the adult student in mind.)

Scales, arpeggios, chords and cadences, etc. are presented too, but whether they are studied intently is left to the discretion of the teacher. Similarly, metronome markings are suggested and should be modified at the teacher's discretion. Though the adult hand is larger than that of the younger student, it does not necessarily follow that octave playing will be easy to do, a common mistake. For that reason octaves are used sparingly and only toward the end of the book.

The Publishers
(1973, updated 2015)

NOTE: This publication is a compilation of what was previously Book 2 and Book 3 of the *Adult Piano Course*.

2nd FINGER CROSSING THE THUMB

Before playing this piece, practice the following exercise until the crossing over of the 2nd finger can be done smoothly. Practice each hand *separately*, the left hand playing one octave lower than written.

Hop O' My Thumb

John Thompson

LEGER LINES

LEGER LINES are *added* lines used above or below the staff.

An easy way to remember leger lines is to note the following:

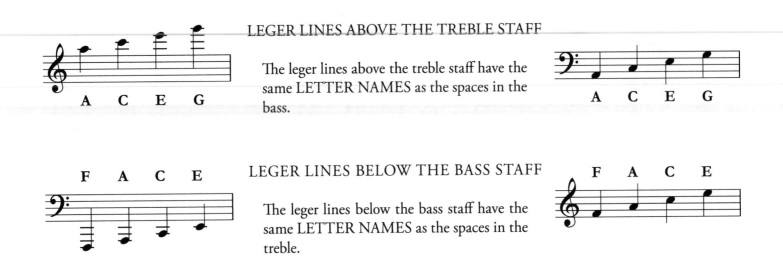

LEGER LINES ABOVE THE TREBLE STAFF

The leger lines above the treble staff have the same LETTER NAMES as the spaces in the bass.

LEGER LINES BELOW THE BASS STAFF

The leger lines below the bass staff have the same LETTER NAMES as the spaces in the treble.

LEGER LINES BETWEEN THE CLEFS

Leger lines between the clefs are *borrowed* lines. In the example below notice how the treble lines are *borrowed* to become leger lines in the bass.

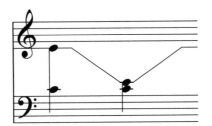

Middle C
Same in both clefs

E }
C } Here the E line of the treble is borrowed and used as a leger line in the bass.

G }
E }
C } Both the E and G lines are borrowed.

The same idea works *in reverse* when borrowing bass lines to use as leger lines in the treble.

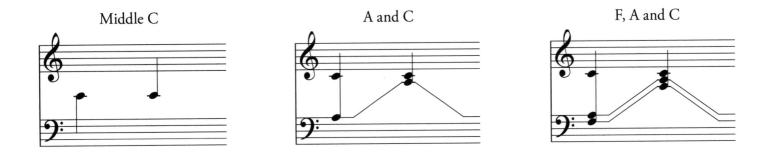

Middle C

A and C

F, A and C

THUMB UNDER THE 2nd FINGER

Before playing this piece, practice the following exercise until the THUMB can be passed under the 2nd finger smoothly *without turning the hand*.

Practice each hand *separately*, the left hand playing one octave lower than written.

Waltz of the Fairies

Schmitt

Allegro moderato (♩ = 184)

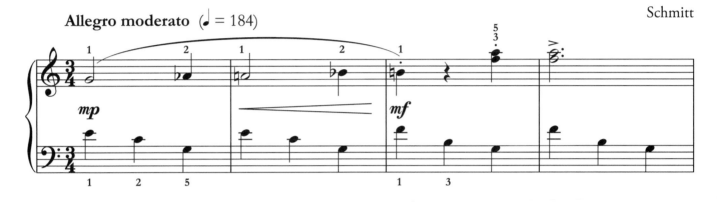

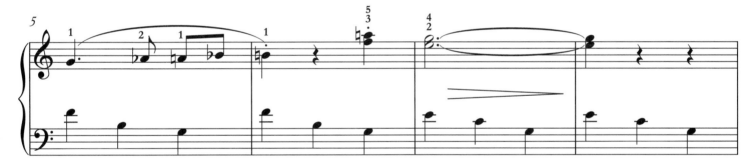

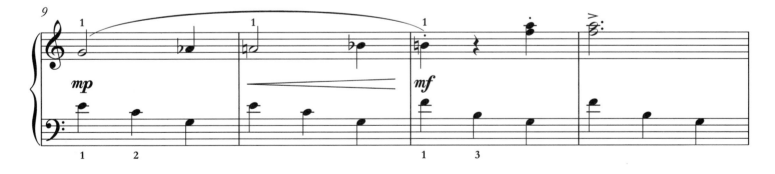

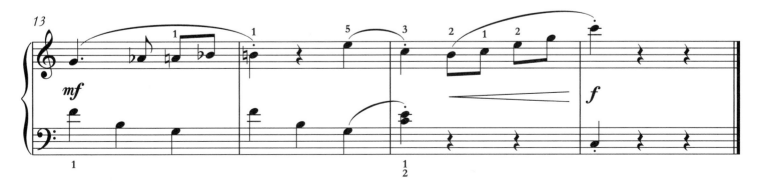

THE PEDAL

There are three pedals on the modern piano.

At present we shall use only the one on the right—the damper pedal.

It is sometimes (incorrectly) called the loud pedal.

Actually it has nothing to do with the loudness of piano playing.

Its function is to *sustain the tone* by raising the dampers from the strings.

There are several markings in use to indicate the pedal.

In this book, this sign L_____J will be used.

The pedal is pressed down at the beginning and released immediately at the end of the sign.

The Beautiful Blue Danube
(Op. 314)

Johann Strauss
1825–1899

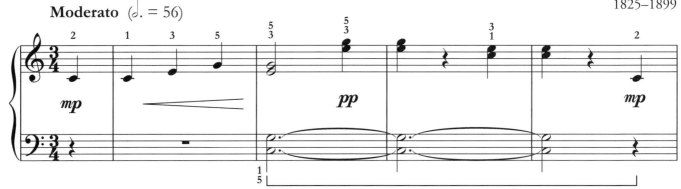

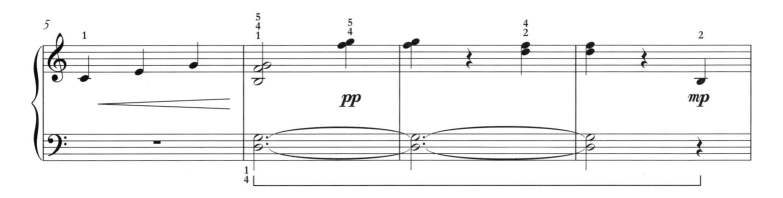

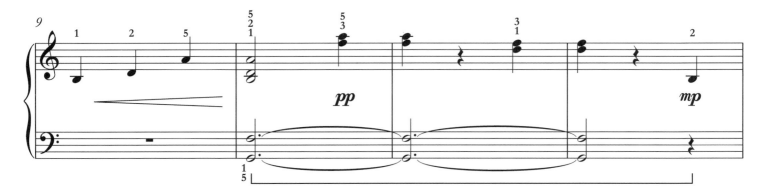

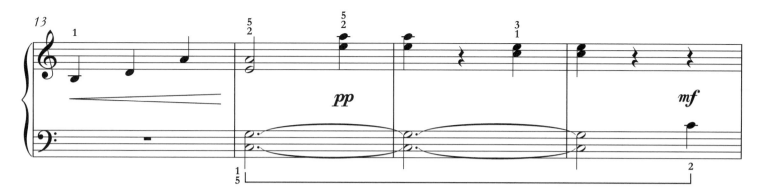

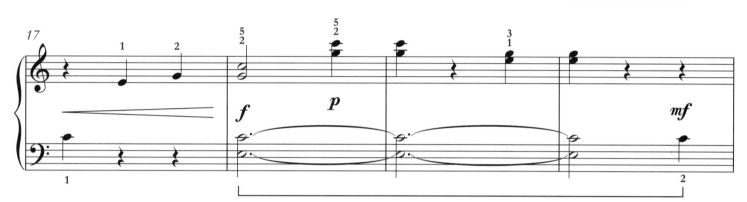

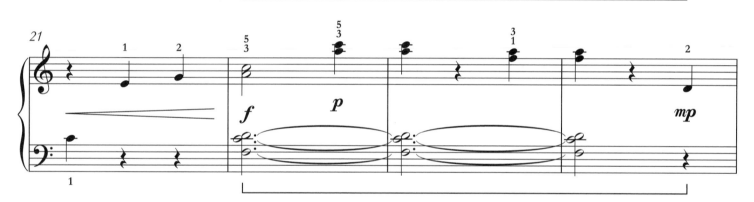

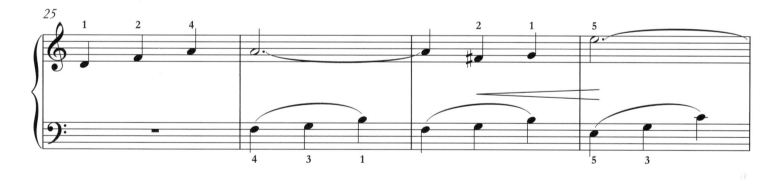

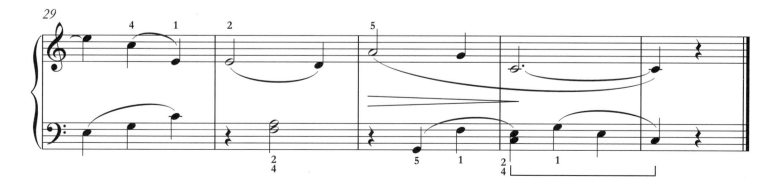

SIGNATURE FOR 4/4

The word *elegy* in literature denotes a poem which is sad and touching. In this music of Massenet's, we find the same feeling.

The sign **C** is used as a time signature to indicate 4/4. It is the modern version of the broken circle **C** which was formerly used.

In the following example, play the left hand melody with your best possible singing tone and subdue the right hand accompanying chords. Pass the thumb smoothly under the 3rd finger.

Elegy
(Op. 10, No. 5)

Jules Massenet
1842–1912

PEDAL POINT

When a bass note is sustained or repeated in measure after measure against other moving harmonies it is known as **pedal point** (or **organ point**).

D is the pedal point in the following number, the well-known "Cradle Song" of Brahms.

Cradle Song
(Op. 49, No. 4)

Johannes Brahms
1833–1897

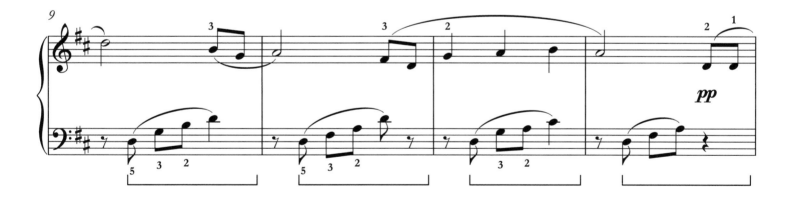

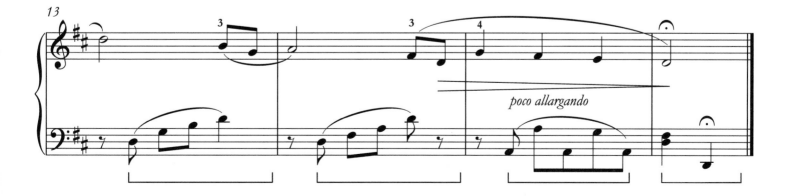

SUSTAINING LOW BASS NOTES IN THE PEDAL

By catching the low note of the bass in the pedal, the left hand is enabled to move up to the next hand position without any noticeable break. This is a device often used in accompaniments.

The Evening Star
from the opera *Tannhauser*

Richard Wagner
1813–1883

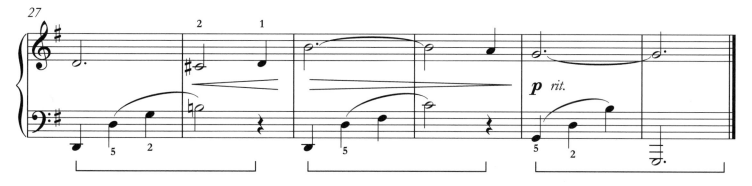

Chord Study
from "Now the Day Is Over"

Joseph Barnby
1838–1896

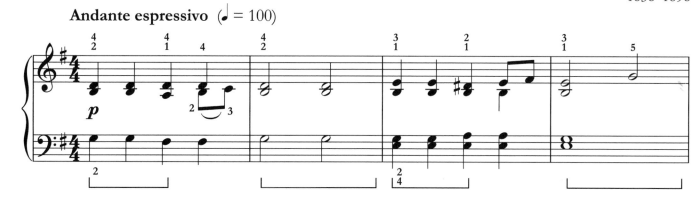

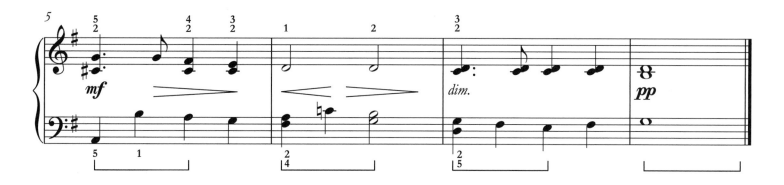

GRACE NOTES

There are several varieties of **grace notes**, but the one most frequently used looks like this:

It has no set time value and should be "flipped" into the principal note as quickly as possible.

Be careful to phrase the two-note slurs properly and make a clear distinction between *forte* and *piano*.

Rondo
(KV 3)

W. A. Mozart
1756–1791

DOUBLE GRACE NOTES

The following theme is from one of the Bach violin sonatas.

In this music we find **double grace notes** which, like single grace notes, have no special time value.

Gavotte
(from BWV 1006)

Johann Sebastian Bach
1685–1750

For those wishing to play more themes from the masters, *John Thompson's Second Year Piano Classics* are recommended. The set includes favorite airs from 14 of the masters, ranging from Bach to Schumann.

THE DOTTED EIGHTH NOTE

The **dotted eighth note** is played exactly the same as the dotted quarter, except it is done in half the time. To get the 'feel' of it, play the following slowly counting "and" on the half beats. Note that the 16th comes *between* "and" and the following count.

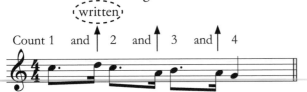

Another way is to count 16ths: i.e. count 4 to each GROUP, playing the 16th on the 4th count.

When playing up to tempo, it is impossible to count fast enough. It may help to think of the 16ths as *grace notes*:

Note how this new rhythmical pattern adds life, sparkle, and verve to this beautiful Old English folk dance.

Country Gardens

Old English Morris Dance

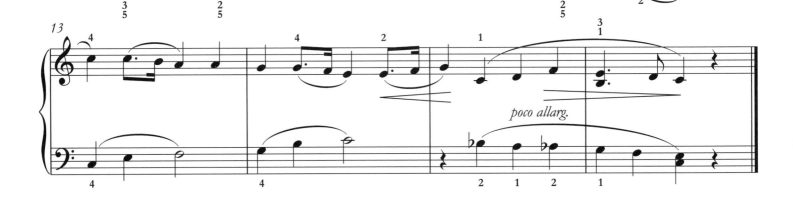

PHRASING—LONG AND SHORT SLURS

Song of India
from the legend *Sadko*

Nikolai Rimsky-Korsakov
1844–1908

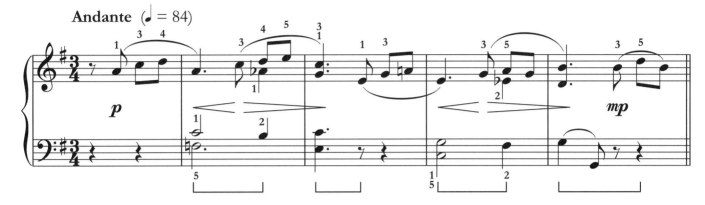

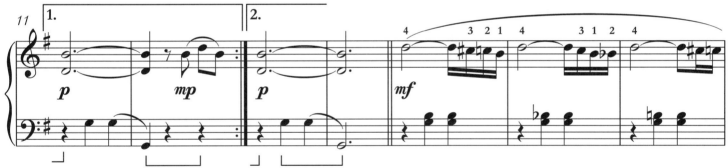

STACCATO NOVELTY

Funeral March of a Marionette

Charles Gounod
1818–1893

Allegro moderato (♩. = 76)

With brittle staccato
mp

Fine

D.C. al Fine

Return to the beginning
and play to *Fine*.

SCALES IN EXTENDED FORM

Scales should now be practiced in extended form (that is, not divided between the hands) for two to four octaves in length.

WRITING BOOKS

For a comprehensive knowledge of scales and chords, the two writing books suggested below are highly recommended.

SCALE-SPELLER
Major, minor and chromatic scales are no problem for the student who uses this book. Intervals are also taught. Easy rules enable the student to identify all scales and intervals *by ear* as well as *by eye*.

CHORD-SPELLER
Major, minor, augmented and diminished triads hold no terrors for the pupil who has mastered intervals in the preceding Speller. Triads with inversions, cadence chords, dominant and diminished sevenths follow in logical order. Again, the student is taught to recognize all chords *by sound* as well as *by sight*.

SCALE STUDY*

Etude

John Thompson

Cheerful and lively ($\quad$ = 112)

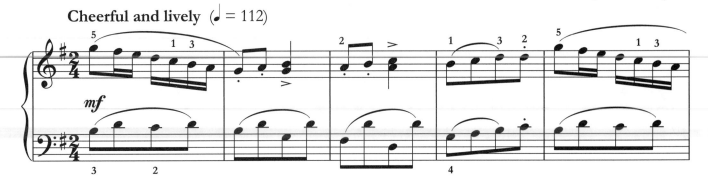

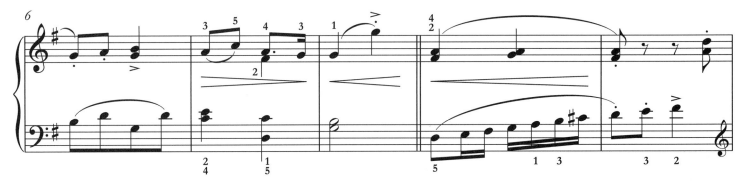

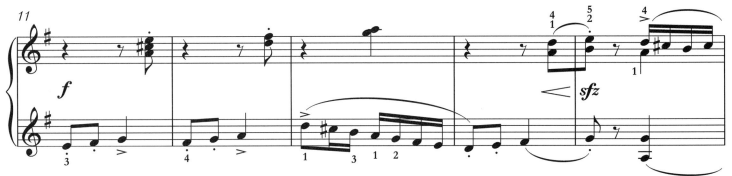

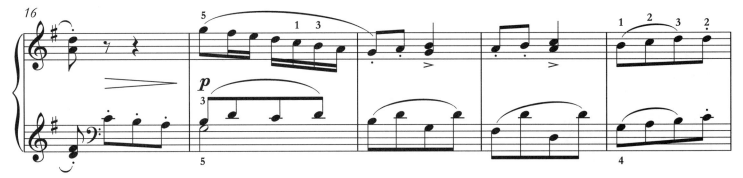

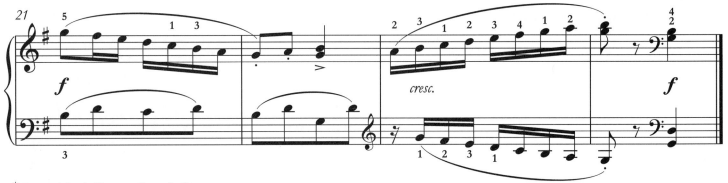

* From *A Little Virtuoso Suite for Piano*

DANCE FORM—THE GAVOTTE

The *gavotte* is an old French dance which always begins on the third count and moves at a moderately fast tempo.

It has been said that the following gavotte was composed by King Louis XIII of France. However, its real origin is uncertain.

Be sure to make strong contrasts between staccato and legato and pass the 3rd finger over as smoothly as possible. Observe all accents and keep an even tempo.

Amaryllis

Attributed to
King Louis XIII
1601–1643

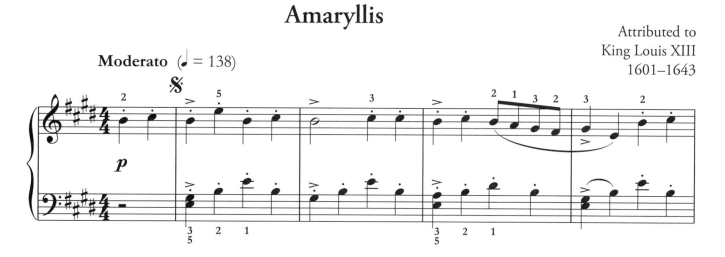

*Return to the sign 𝄋 and play to *Fine*.

NEW PEDAL MARK

This sign └──⋀──⋀──┘ is used to show that the pedal is released and pressed down again immediately in order to preserve an unbroken legato. It is used frequently in chord playing.

Carry Me Back to Old Virginny

James A. Bland
1854–1911

ARPEGGIO

A broken chord is called an **arpeggio**.

Arpeggio is an Italian word meaning "in the style of a harp."

The following etude consists of arpeggios divided between the hands. Play as smoothly as possible and try to make the broken chords sound as though played with one hand.

Etude

Carl Czerny
1791–1857

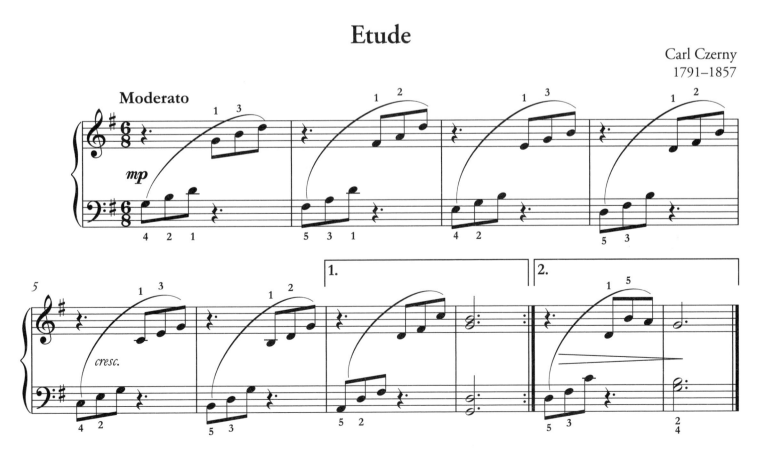

THE BROKEN CHORD MARK

When a wavy line is placed before a chord, such as those shown in the following example, it means the chord is to be "broken"—quickly, as though the lower notes were written as grace notes.

The right hand melody must be played as *legato* as possible against the *staccatos* of the left hand which represent the *pizzicato* of the violin, for which this piece was originally written.

Orientale

César Cui
1835–1918

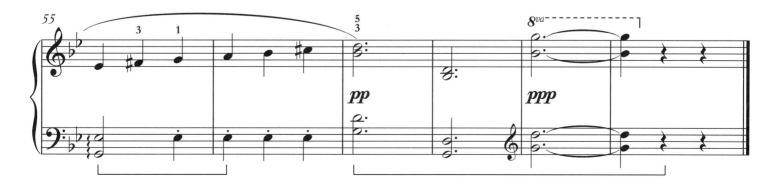

FINGER FLUENCY

In this piece the right hand is legato throughout against two-note slurs in the left hand.

Practice first at a slow tempo, then increase the speed as finger fluency develops.

Valse
(Op. 83)

Marie-Auguste Durand
1830–1909

TRIPLETS

A *triplet* is a group of three notes (or chords) played in the time normally given to two notes of the same value.

It is indicated: ♩♩♩ or ♩♩♩

In the following example the three eighth notes in each triplet will be played **on one count**.

Symphony No. 5
(Theme from 2nd movement)

Pyotr Ilyich Tchaikovsky
1840–1893

Andante cantabile (♩ = 84)

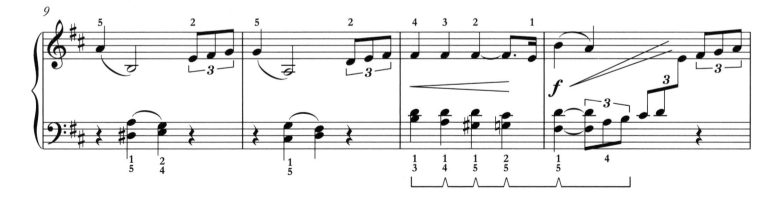

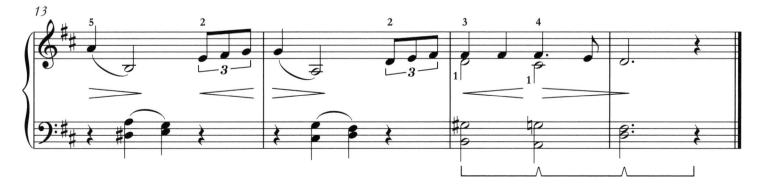

SYNCOPATION

When an accent is taken away from a strong beat and placed on a weak beat, the normal rhythmical flow is disturbed and the result is known as *syncopation*. In the following example, all syncopated beats are shown by a little black triangle: ▼ . Syncopation can be produced in three ways: the TIE, the LONG NOTE or the REST. Count aloud at first, using the word "and" on the half beats shown by this sign: + .

Shortnin' Bread

Spiritual

For those wishing to make a further study of syncopation—its cause and effect—John Thompson's *Syncopation Made Easy*, Books 1 and 2 are recommended. The above example is from Book 1.

CROSSING THE THUMB OVER IN ARPEGGIO PLAYING

First practice each hand separately, then hands together.

Etude

STACCATO 3rds and 6ths

Etude

Jean-Baptiste Duvernoy
1802–1880

NOCTURNE FORM

Liebestraum No. 3

(Theme)

Franz Liszt
1811–1886

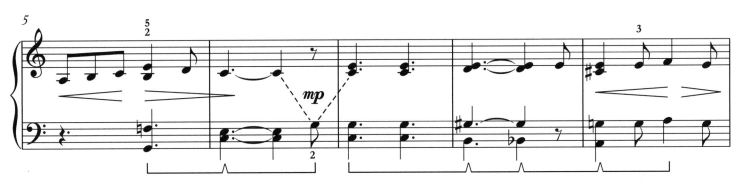

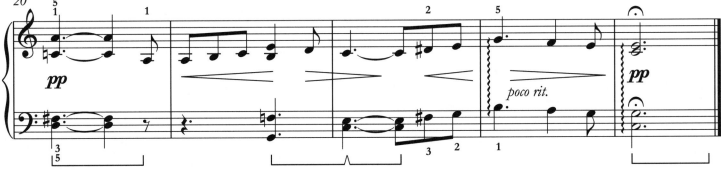

THE TRILL

The trill is an ornamental figure which is very effective when well performed. It consists of an alternating shake between the principal note (the note written) and the next note above. The early keyboard instruments had very little sustaining qualities and the trill was used originally to give the effect of a long, sustained tone. The number of notes played in a trill is entirely left to the choice of the performer. While "Spinning Wheel" does not contain any trills, the notation in the left hand emulates an even, balanced trill. (See page 77 of Book 1.)

Spinning Wheel*

Fritz Spindler
1817–1905

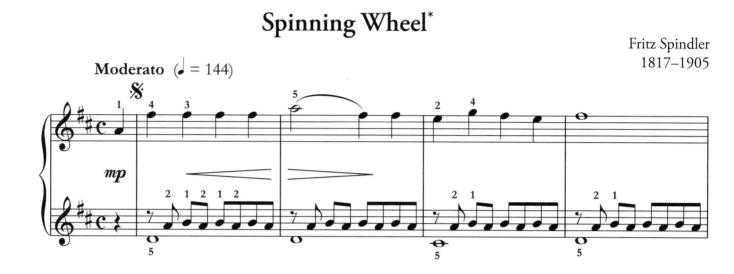

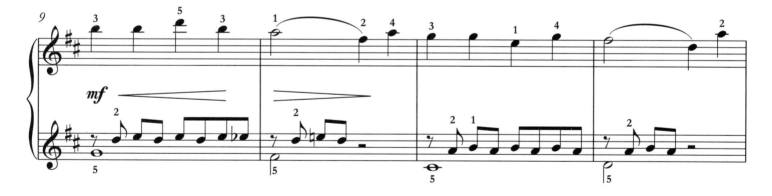

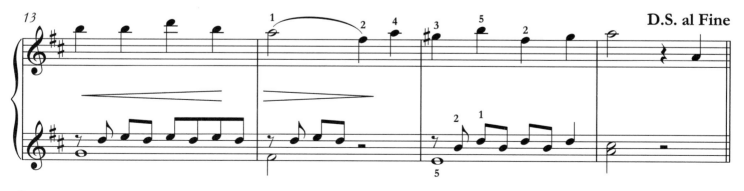

* From *Studies in Style* by John Thompson

STUDY IN STYLE

Valse
(Op. 18)

Frédéric Chopin
1810–1849

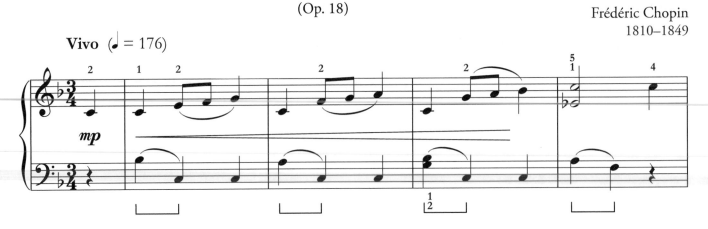

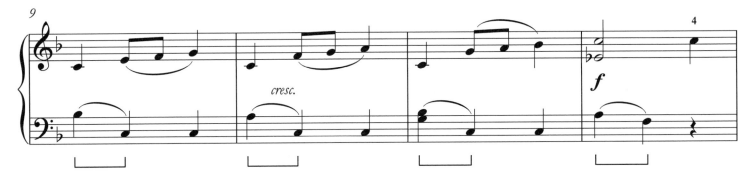

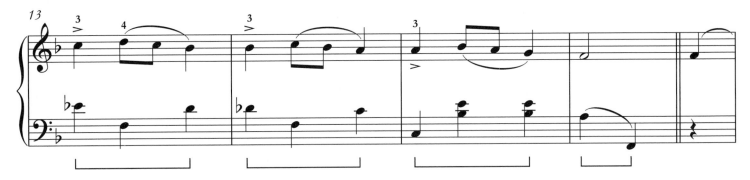

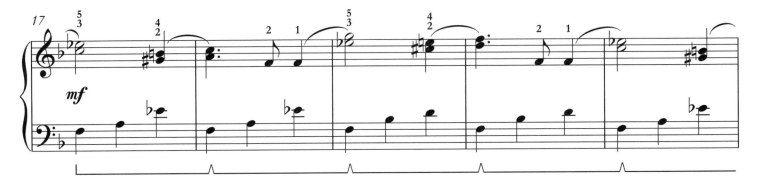

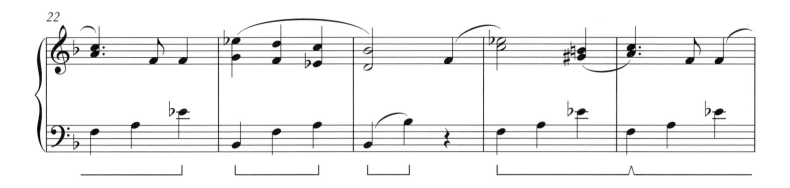

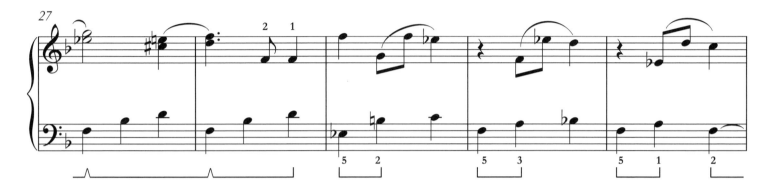

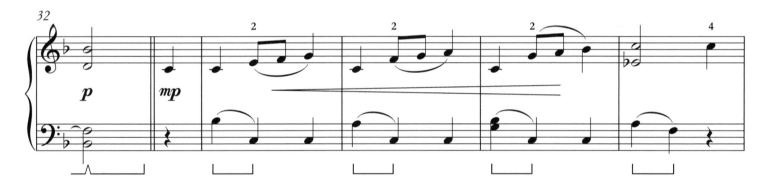

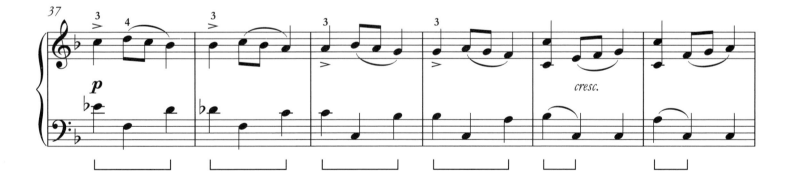

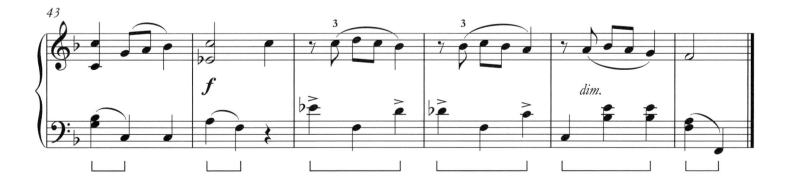

GRAND OPERA

Anvil Chorus
from the opera *Il trovatore*

Giuseppe Verdi
1813–1901

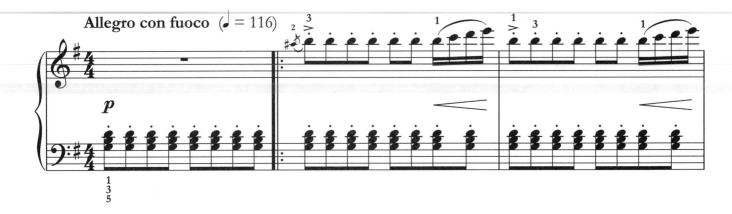

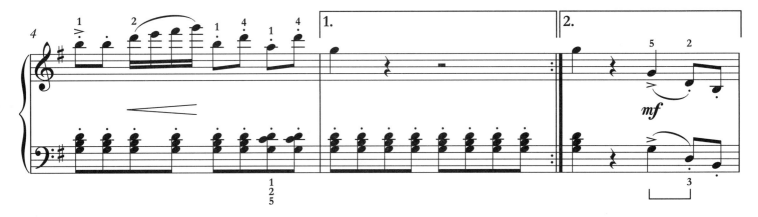

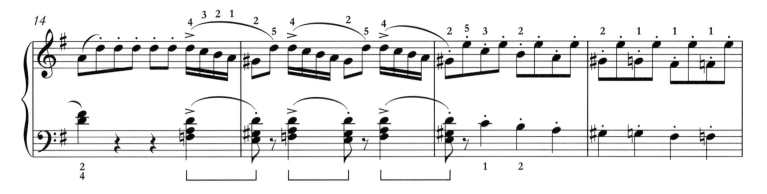

Allegro maestoso

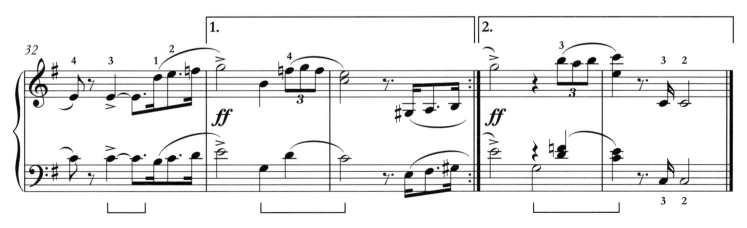

CROSS-HAND PLAYING

Narcissus
from *Water Scenes*, Op. 13

Ethelbert Nevin
1862–1901

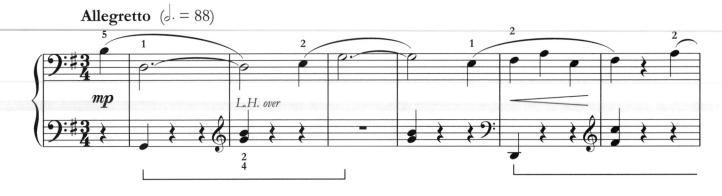

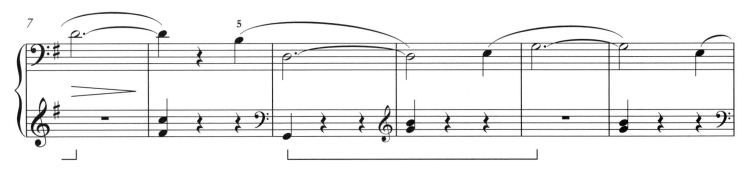

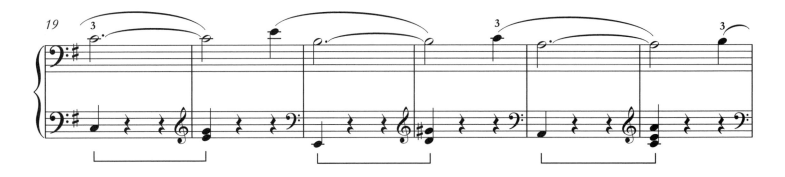

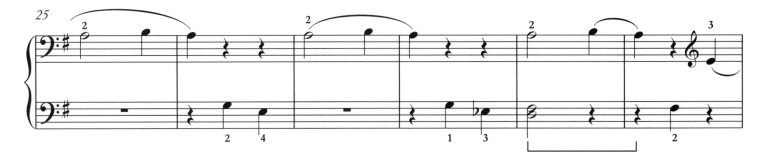

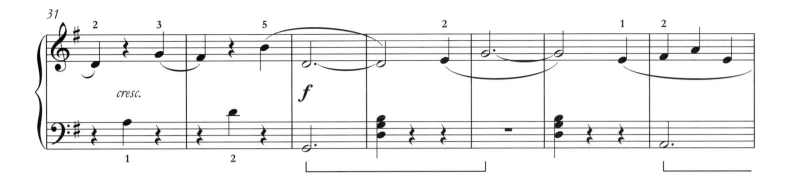

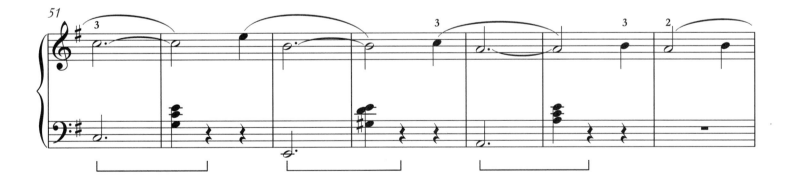

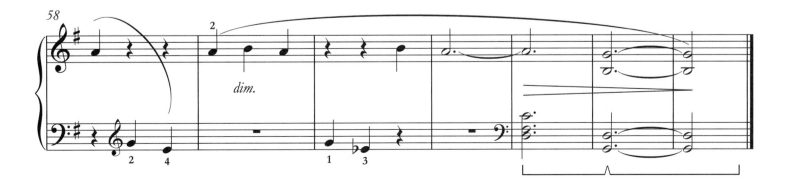

ARPEGGIO ACCOMPANIMENT

Spring Song
(Op. 62, No. 6)

Felix Mendelssohn
1809–1847

Allegretto grazioso ($\quad$ = c.132)

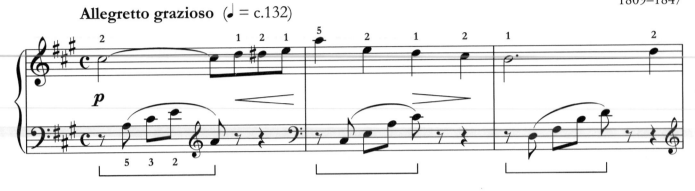

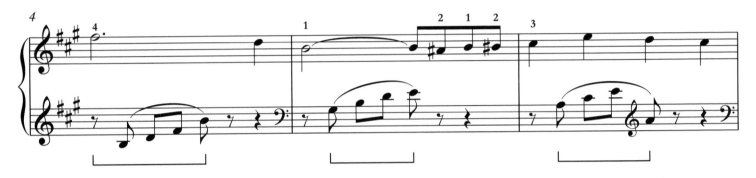

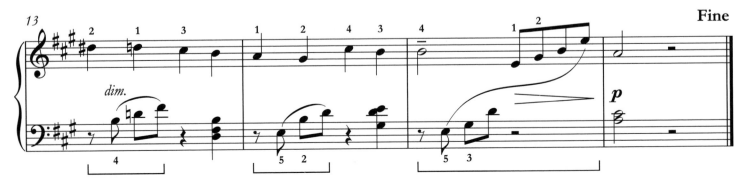

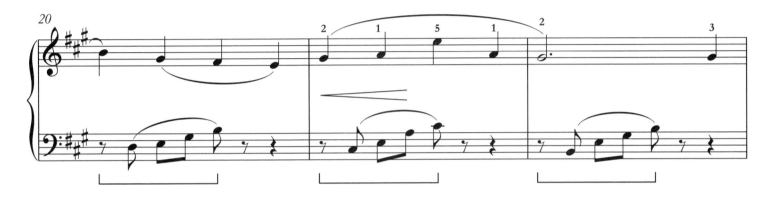

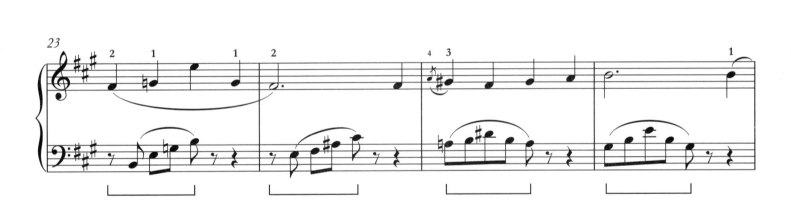

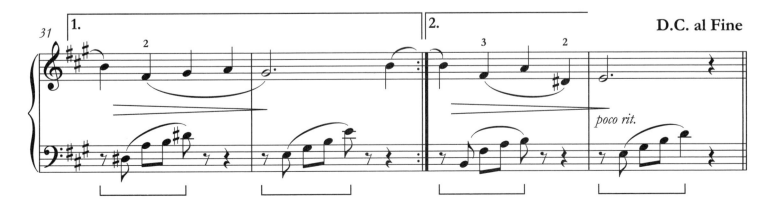

ALLA BREVE

This sign ₵ is called **alla breve** and is used to indicate $\frac{2}{2}$ which means there will be TWO counts to each measure and ONE count to each HALF NOTE.

However, learn the piece first in $\frac{4}{4}$, counting four as usual. As speed develops, reduce the count to two: one count to each half note.

Concerto in A Minor
(Theme from 1st Movement, Op. 16)

Edvard Grieg
1843–1907

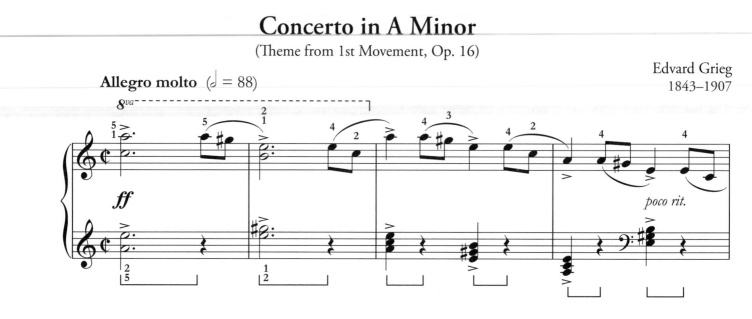

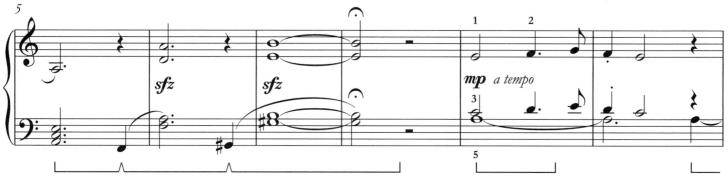

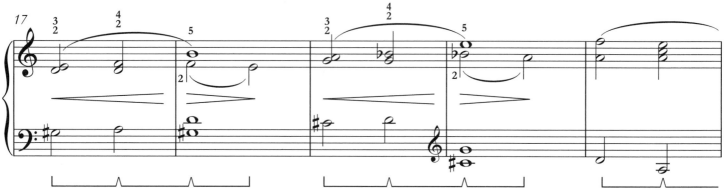

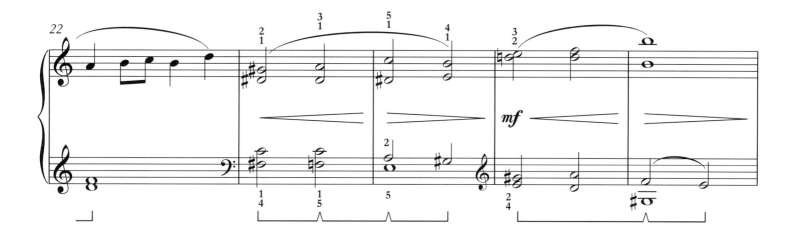

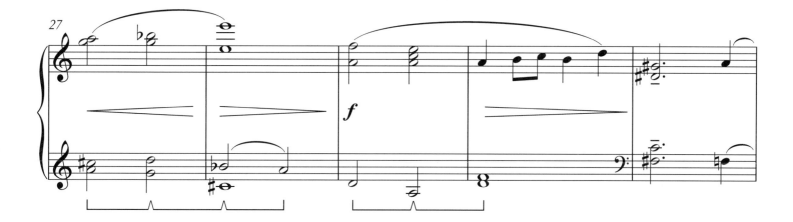

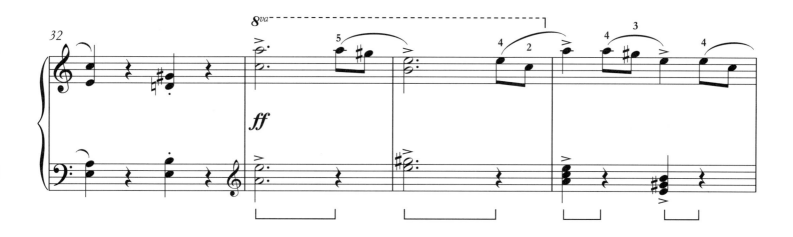

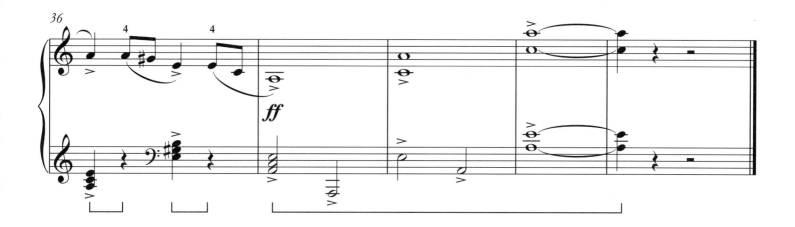

THE DOUBLE-SHARP SIGN

This is the sign of the **double-sharp**: ✗ . It means that the notes before which it is placed must be raised TWO half steps. You will have some "white sharps" in this piece, i.e. E♯, B♯ and the double-sharps which fall on white keys.

Don't allow the 6-sharp key signature to cause any concern. The left hand part is pretty much the same throughout. Just remember to play everything sharp but B (with one exception), and all will be well. When learned, you will have in your fingers one of the most beautiful melodies ever penned.

Romance
(Op. 28, No. 2)

Robert Schumann
1810–1856

Semplice (♩ = 88)

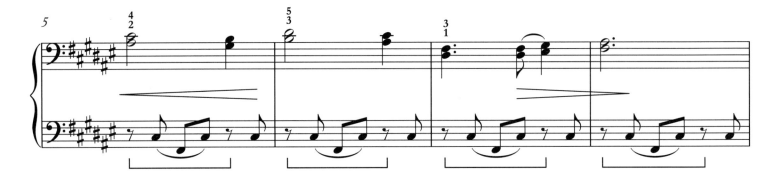

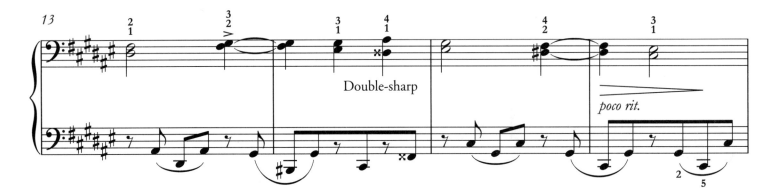

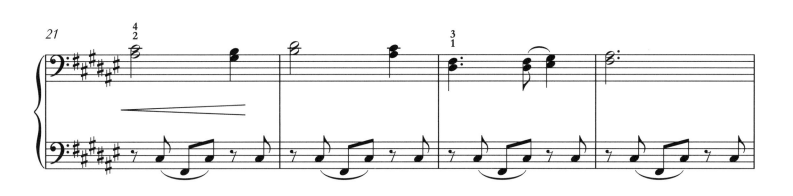

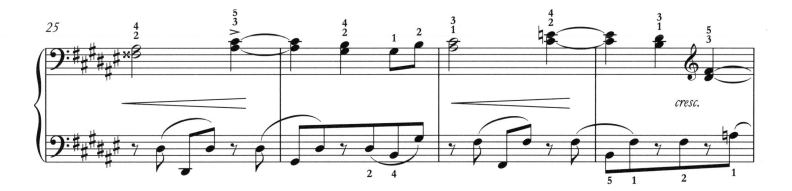

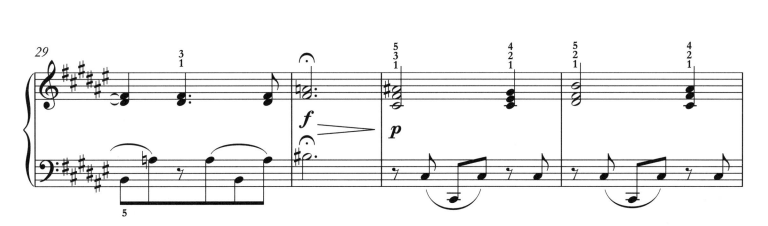

STACCATO

Two Guitars

Traditional Gypsy Tune

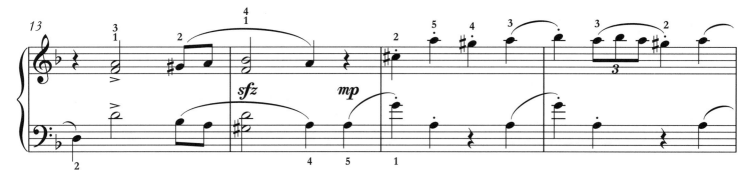

FOR LEFT HAND ALONE

Meditation

John Thompson

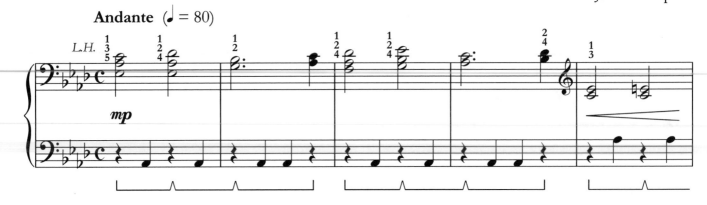

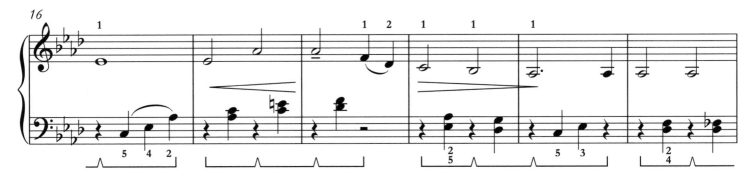

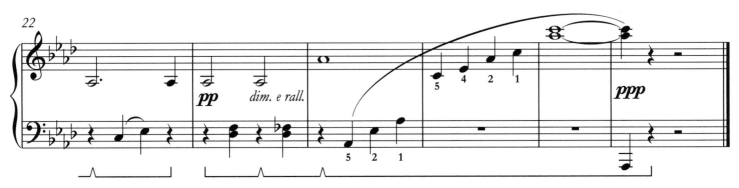

CROSS-HAND and TWO-NOTE SLURS

Be sure to apply the "drop-roll" touch to all two-note slurs. This will produce a rhythmical "swing" suggesting swaying palms. Cross the left hand over gracefully and pedal as marked.

Palms in the Moonlight

John Thompson

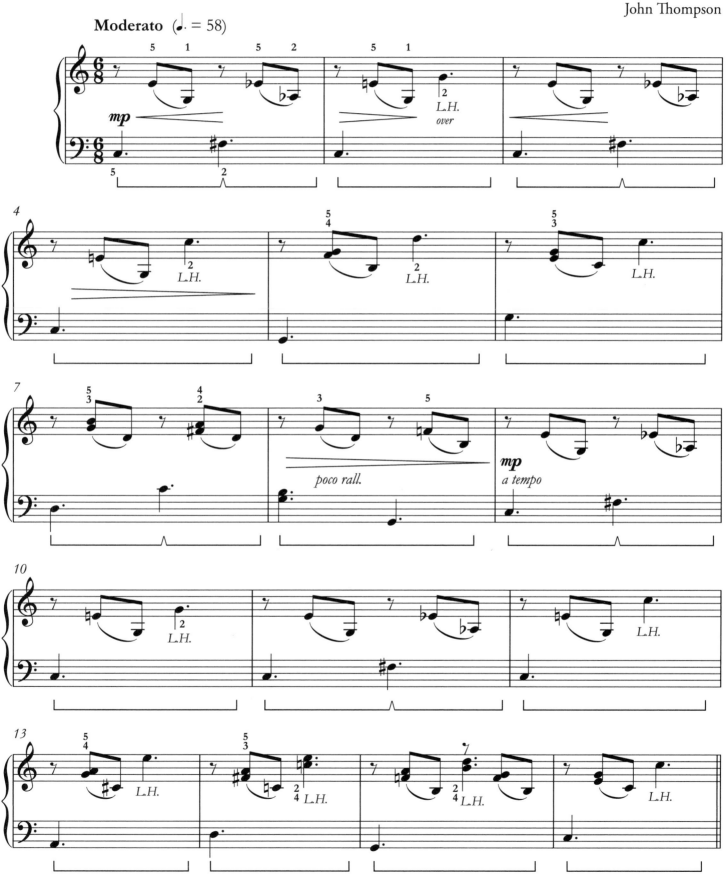

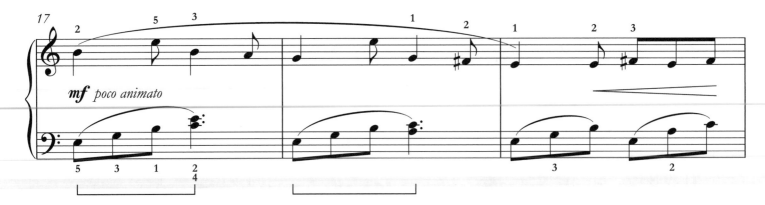

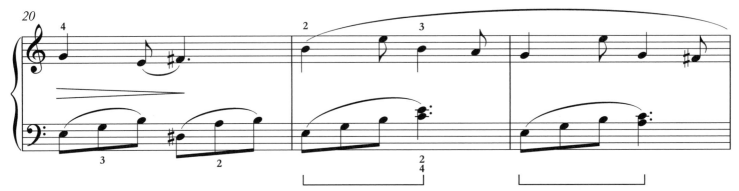

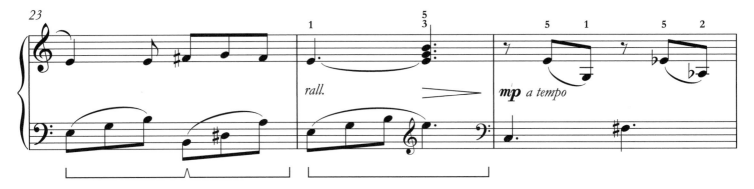

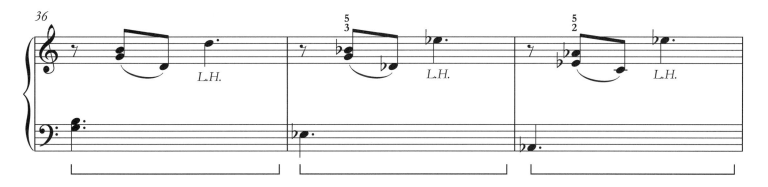

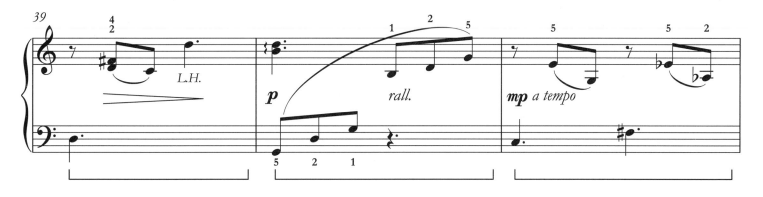

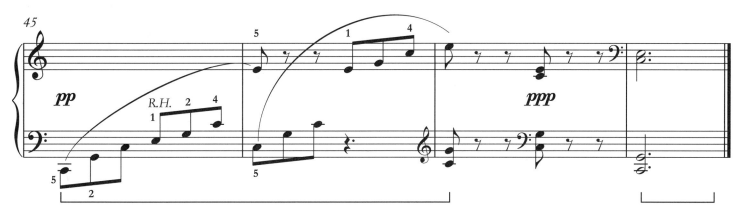

SHARP CONTRASTS IN TEMPO

The following example is typical of Hungarian gypsy music. The first section is played in song style, rather pensive in mood. Later, without warning, it plunges into a fiery dance played *Presto*. Preserve a well-defined rhythm throughout. It was the custom for those not engaged in playing or dancing to beat the rhythm on pots and pans. Therefore, sharp accents are indicated.

Hungarian Dance

Traditional Folk Dance

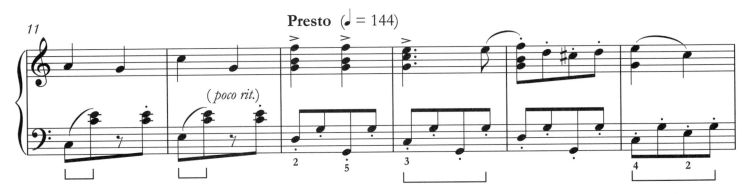

TEACHING THE MINOR SCALES

There are two distinct approaches to teaching the **minor scales**: (1) the **relative** minor; (2) the **parallel** minor. Although each method has decided merit, teachers differ in the choice of approach. For that reason both methods have been presented in the following pages and either may be used according to preference.

WHY DIFFERENT METHODS ARE USED

Teachers who use the **relative** minor approach do so because the key signature remains the same for both major and minor.

The **parallel** minor approach is used because it causes less complication in the matter of fingering—especially in the **white key minors**, where the fingering remains exactly the same as in the **parallel majors**. However, the student should know *both* approaches. For instance, after having played G Major, the student should be able at once to play either G Minor or E Minor with equal facility. A debate, therefore, on the merits of either approach is rather useless.

HARMONIC MINOR FIRST

In the opinion of the author it seems unwise to attempt teaching all three forms of the minor (to the average student) at once. An old rule: "One thing at a time," is quite applicable to minor scales. Experience proves that if the harmonic form is learned first in *all* keys, the result is one of less confusion and more perfect mastery, both analytical and technical, on the part of the student. Afterwards, when the scales are being reviewed for the second time, the other forms of the minor may be taught, thus showing the evolution of the minor scale from **natural** to **melodic** to **harmonic**.

See chart on pages 88 and 89.

FORMING MINOR SCALES
The Relative Minor approach

Every major scale has a *Relative Minor* scale.

The Relative Minor scale begins on the sixth degree of the major scale.

There are three forms of the minor scale: NATURAL minor, MELODIC minor and HARMONIC minor.

For the present we shall consider only the HARMONIC minor.

The Harmonic Minor is formed from the (Relative) Major Scale by *raising the seventh note* (of the minor scale) *one half step.*

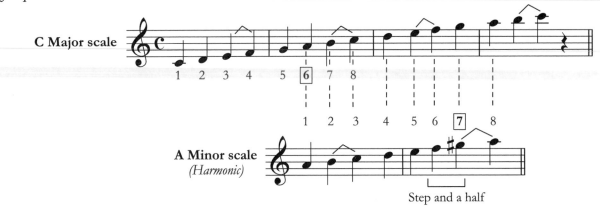

A Minor is *relative* to C Major.

The fingering for A Minor is the same as that for A Major.

Observe that the minor scale employs the same notes as the (Relative) major scale—*except the seventh*, which is raised *one half step.*

A minor key has the *same signature* as the Relative Major Key.

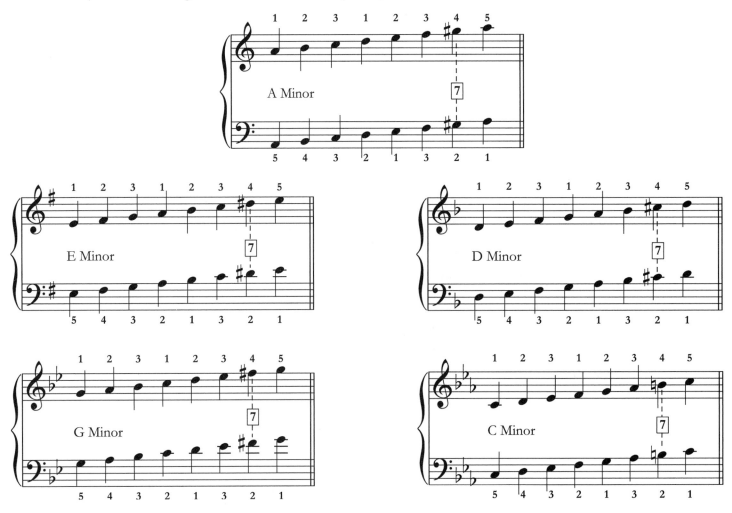

NOTE: Teachers who prefer to teach all three forms of the minor scale at this point should use the chart on pages 88 and 89.

FORMING MINOR SCALES
The Parallel Minor approach

Every major scale has a *Parallel Minor* scale.

The Parallel Minor scale begins on the *same note* as the Major scale.

There are three forms of the minor scale: NATURAL minor, MELODIC minor and HARMONIC minor.

For the present we shall consider only the HARMONIC minor.

The Harmonic Minor is formed from the (Parallel) Major Scale by *lowering the 3rd and 6th degrees one half step.*

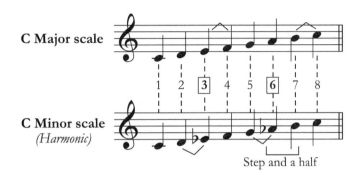

C Minor is *parallel* to C Major.

The fingering remains the same as in the major scale.

Observe that the lowered notes always occur at the point where the *3rd fingers play together.* (This rule applies for the first five WHITE KEY minor scales, i.e. C, G, D, A, E.)

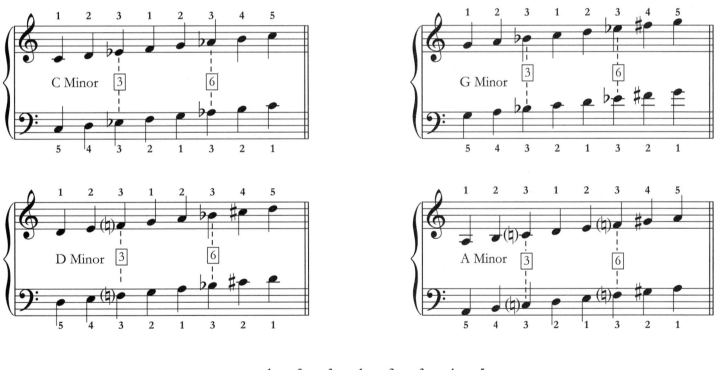

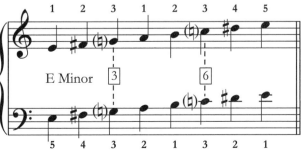

MAJOR AND MINOR MODES

Note that the first theme of this piece is in the key of C Major and that the second theme is in the key of
A Minor, relative to C Major. This is but another illustration of the Law of Contrast—the first law of all art.

A Journey in the Arctic

John Thompson

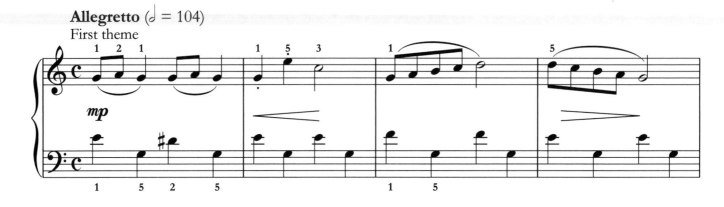

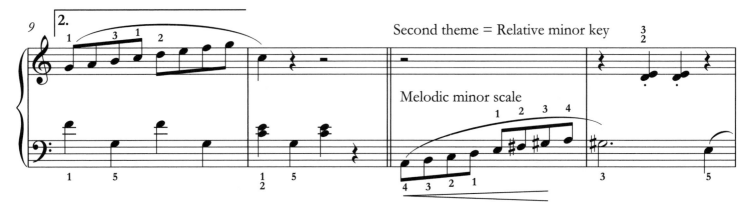

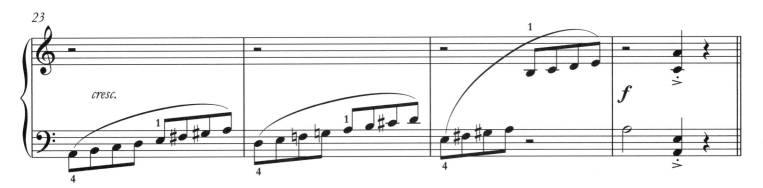

PARALLEL MAJOR AND MINOR KEYS

The following is an example of parallel major and minor keys. The piece begins in A Minor and later goes into its parallel major—the key of A Major.

La Cinquantaine
(The Golden Wedding)

Jean Gabriel Marie
1852–1928

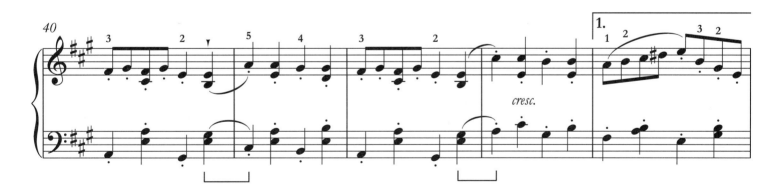

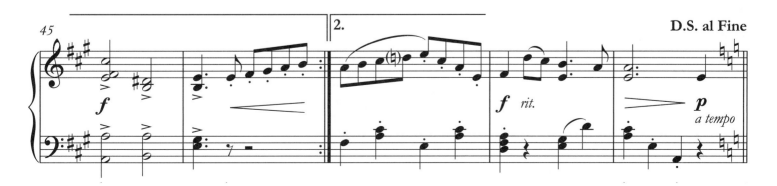

Like so many of MacDowell's miniatures, the charm of this piece lies in its utter simplicity. Strive to give it as much color as possible without creating too much emotional excitement—not always easy! Perhaps the very best key to interpretation will be found in MacDowell's own words: "With simple tenderness." Pedal once to each measure except where otherwise marked.

To a Wild Rose

Edward MacDowell
1860–1908

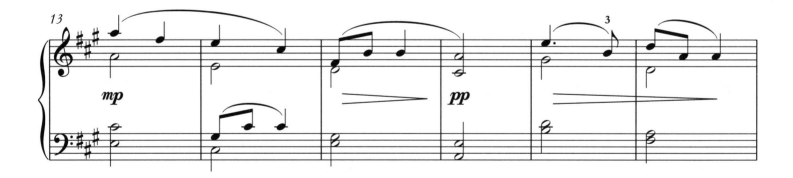

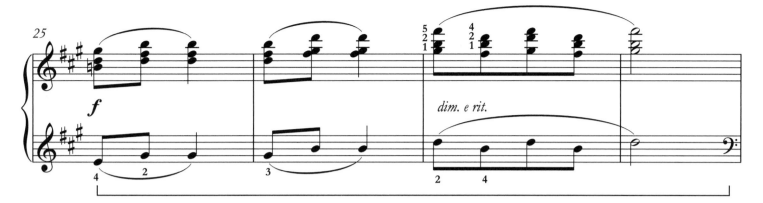

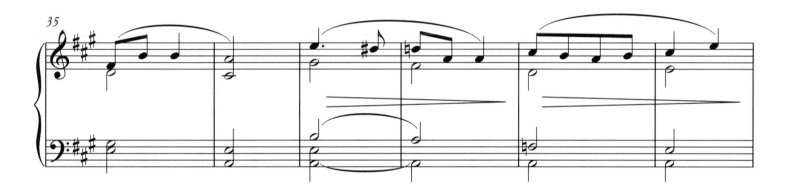

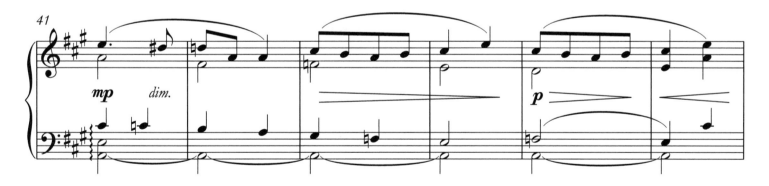

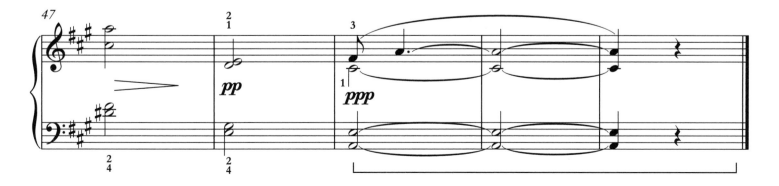

Note that the following "Etude in G Minor" bears the same key signature as its relative major (B-flat Major). Both forms of the minor scale are shown—the melodic minor being used on the last line.

Etude in G Minor

John Thompson

Dolores

Émile Waldteufel
1837–1915

Moderato con moto (= 58)

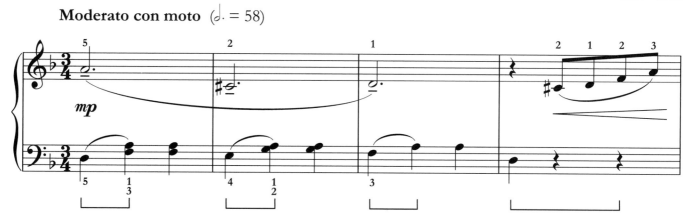

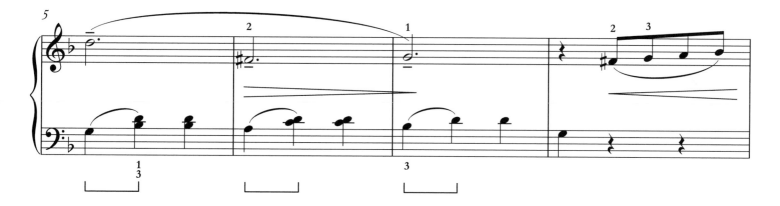

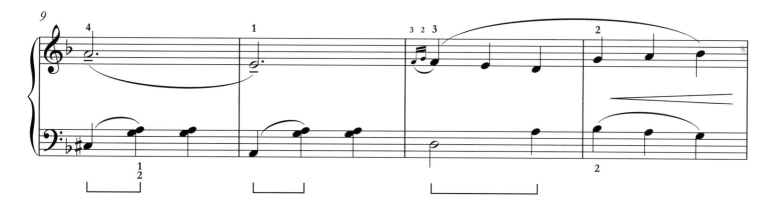

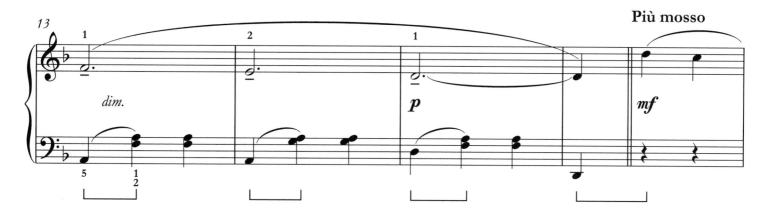

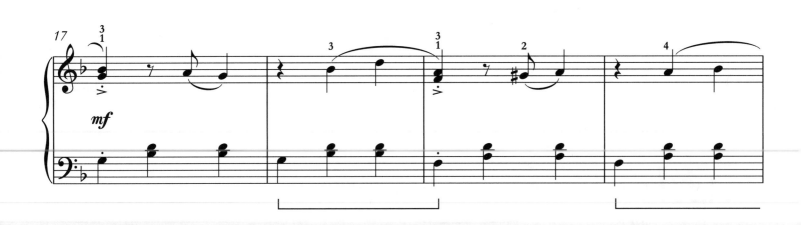

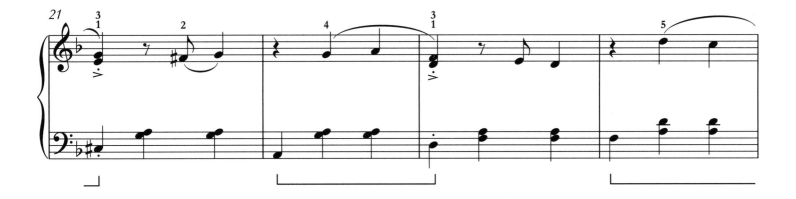

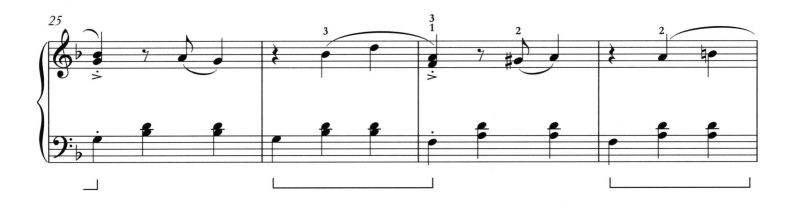

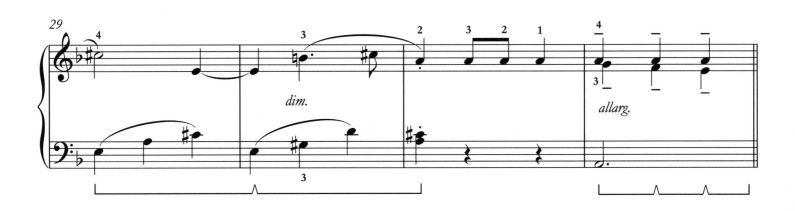

Tempo I

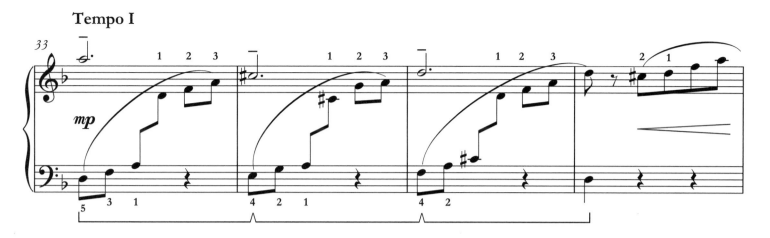

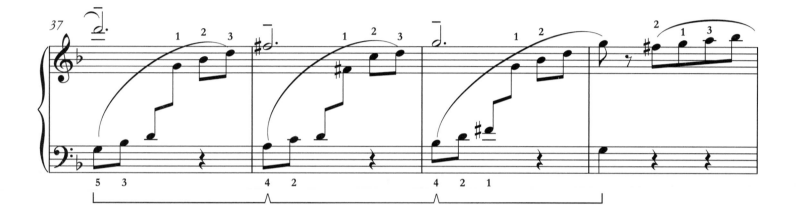

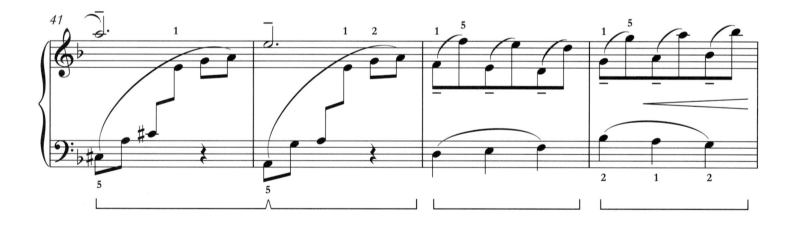

From old Vienna, the Austrian city of melody, comes this wistful song, transcribed here for piano. Play it with sympathetic expression, following phrasing and expression marks closely and using the pedal exactly as indicated. A good singing tone is essential.

A Viennese Melody

Folk Tune

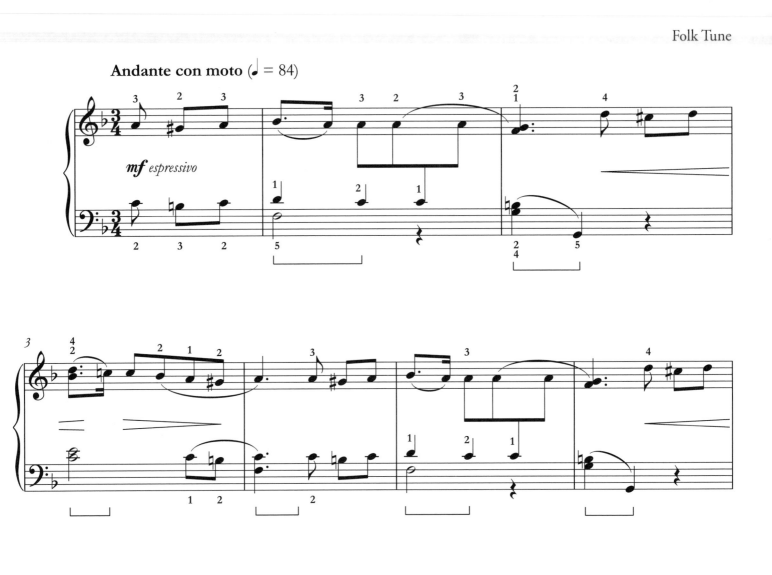

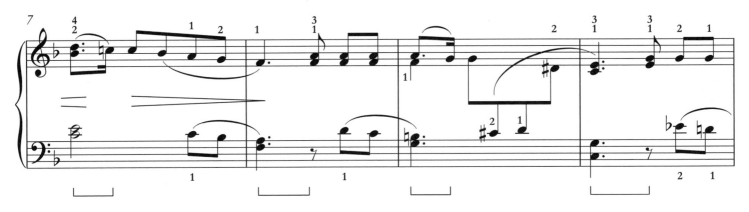

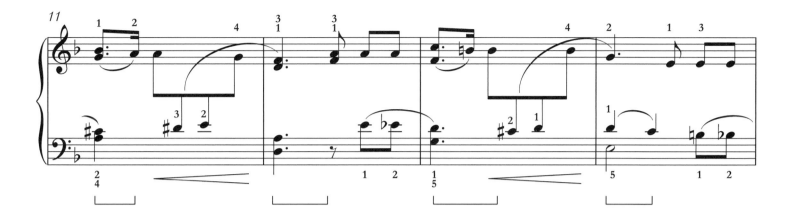

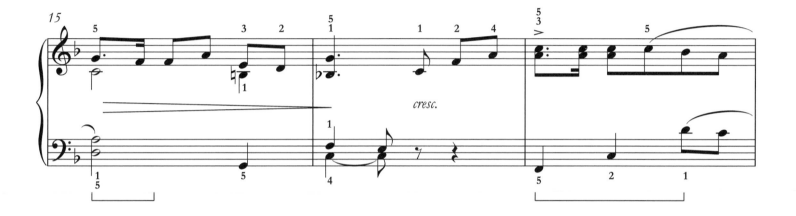

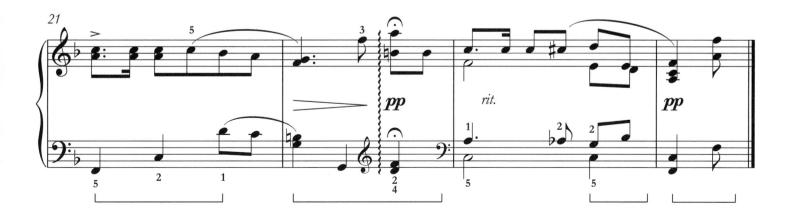

UP-ARM STROKE AND ARM IMPULSE

In this preparatory exercise, play all staccato chords with an up-arm stroke. Play both chords enclosed in brackets with a bouncing one-arm-impulse. Apply the same technique to "Dark Eyes," playing the accented chords with an up-arm stroke and the two following chords on a single-arm impulse.

Preparatory Study

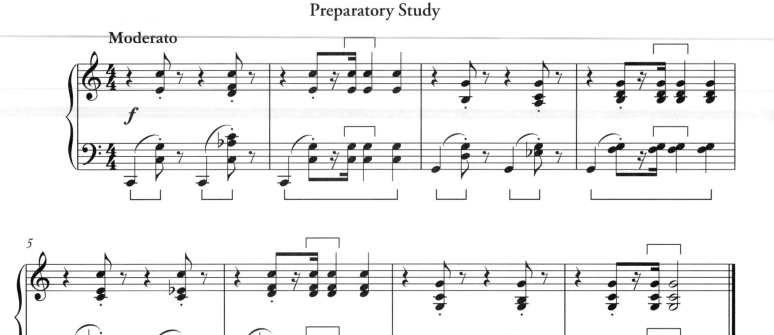

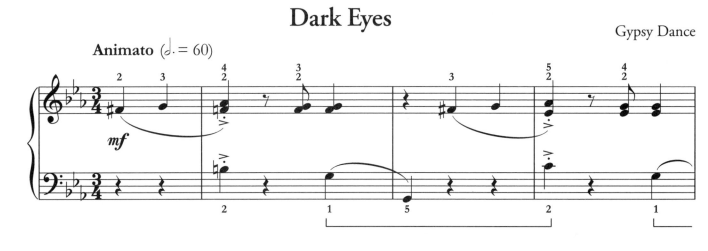

Play the following with free, fiery abandon characteristic of gypsy dances, employing sharp accents and staccato.

Dark Eyes

Gypsy Dance

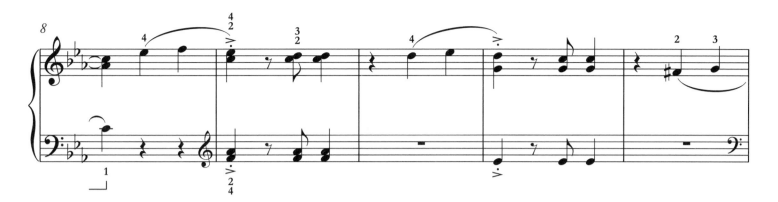

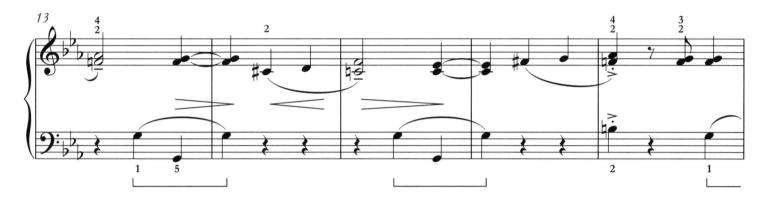

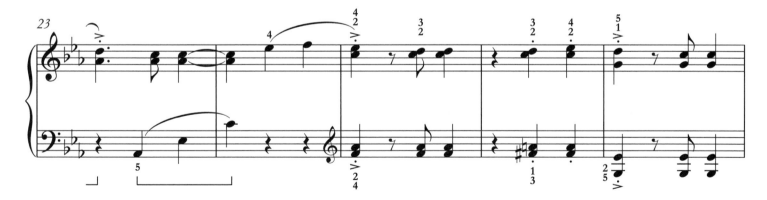

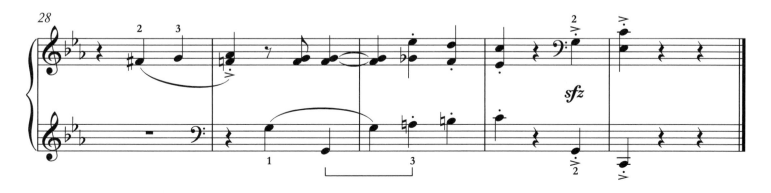

This beautiful, impressionistic piece of Debussy's is immensely popular among all classes of music lovers. It calls for the most delicate treatment possible in handling the dissonances which are sometimes purposely sustained with the pedal.

The changes in time signatures need offer no hazard if one remembers to give exactly the same value to a quarter note, whether it be in a measure of **2/4** or **3/4** .

Clair de Lune

Claude Debussy
1862–1918

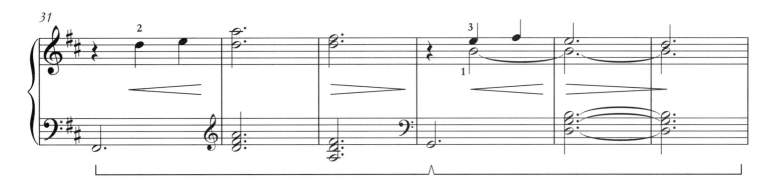

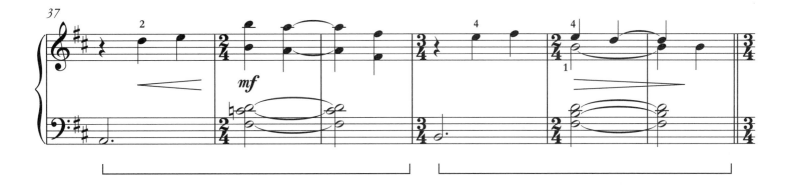

Tempo rubato

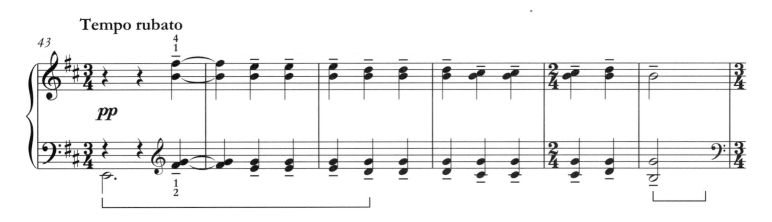

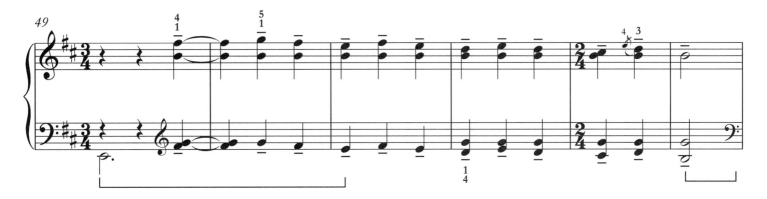

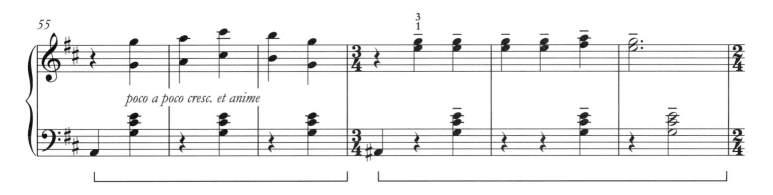

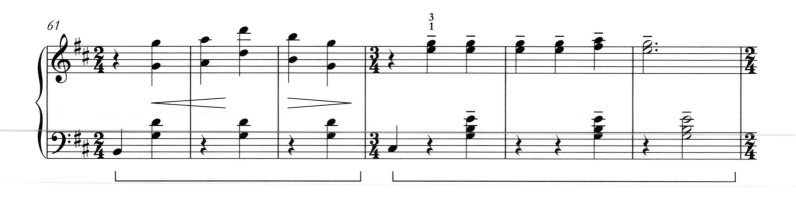

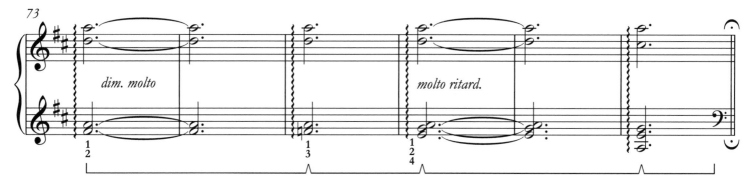

Tempo I

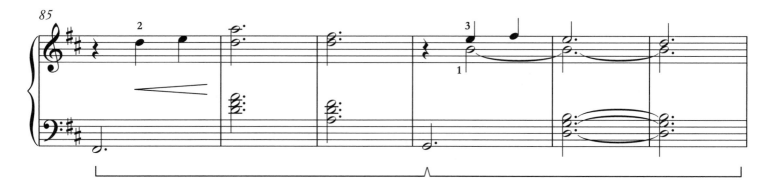

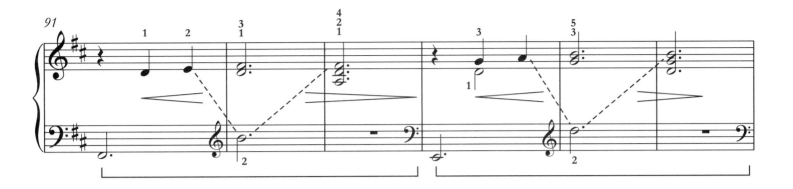

CADENCE CHORDS

What a period is to a sentence, a cadence is to music. In other words, a *cadence* is the end of a musical sentence.

The principal triads of the scale are those found on the FIRST, FOURTH and FIFTH degrees.
They are important because they are the chords used in forming *cadences*.

These chords are named TONIC, SUBDOMINANT and DOMINANT as shown below.

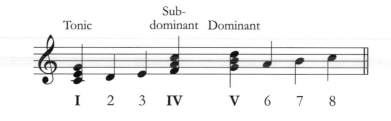

Study

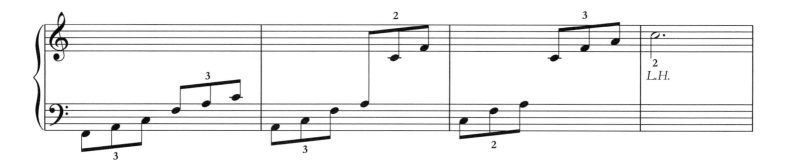

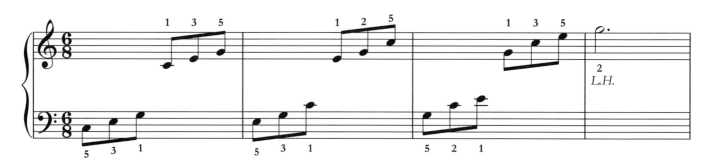

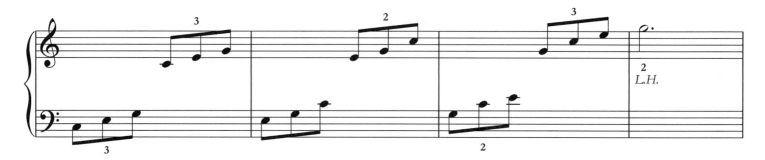

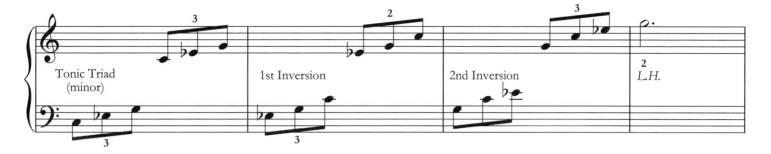

Tonic Triad (minor) — 1st Inversion — 2nd Inversion — L.H.

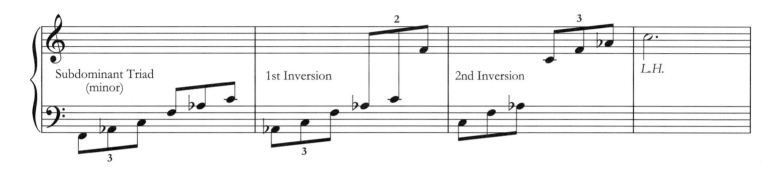

Subdominant Triad (minor) — 1st Inversion — 2nd Inversion — L.H.

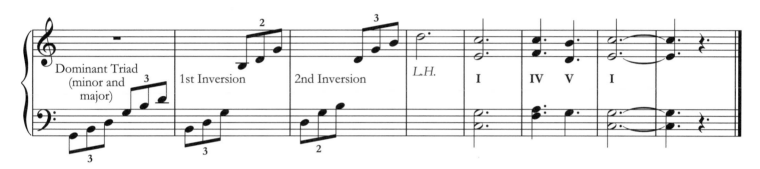

Dominant Triad (minor and major) — 1st Inversion — 2nd Inversion — L.H. — I — IV — V — I

Familiar Cadences

Tonic and Dominant Chords

I V I   I V I   I V I

i V i   i V i   i V i

Tonic and Subdominant Chords

I IV I   I IV I   I IV I

i iv i   i iv i   i iv i

Tonic, Dominant and Subdominant Chords

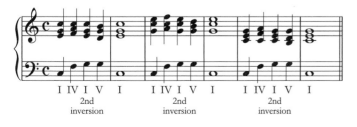

I IV IV V I   I IV IV V I   I IV IV V I
2nd inversion

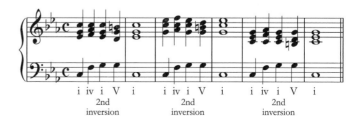

i iv iv V i   i iv iv V i   i iv iv V i
2nd inversion

THE DOMINANT SEVENTH CHORD

The triad on the fifth degree of the scale (the dominant) often appears with an added 7th and is known as the *Chord of the Dominant Seventh*. Because it contains four notes, three inversions are possible.

Santa Lucia

Neapolitan Boat Song

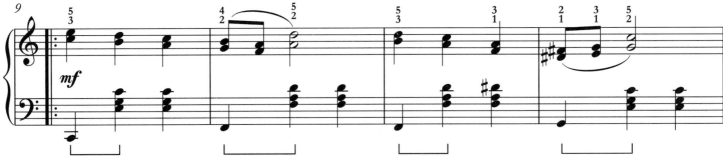

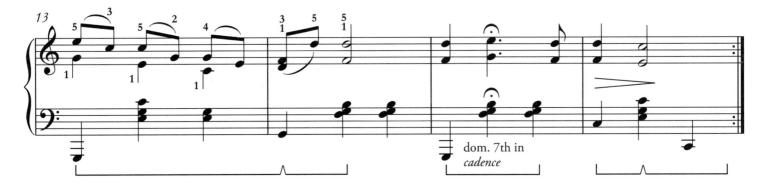

THE DOMINANT SEVENTH ARPEGGIO

Practice the above, first each hand separately, then together an octave apart.

Juanita

Spanish Folk Tune

Etude

John Thompson

Allegro

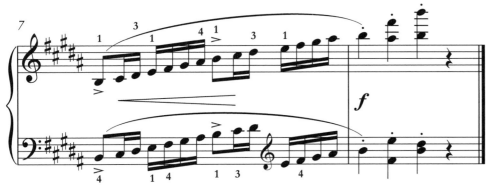

Transposition.

After memorizing this etude, see how many different keys you can play it in. You might also try to transpose it into minor keys.

Mighty Lak' a Rose

Ethelbert Nevin
1862–1901

Simply ($\quarternote$ = 66)

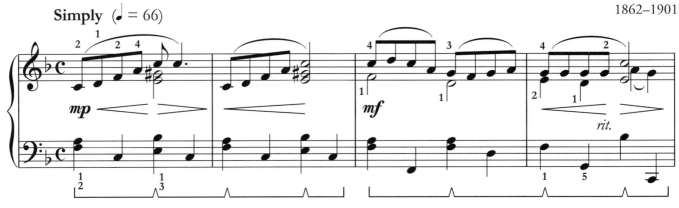

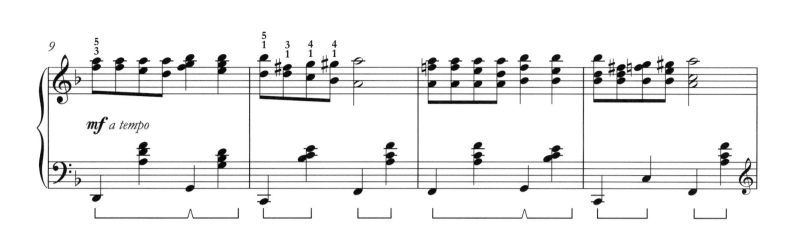

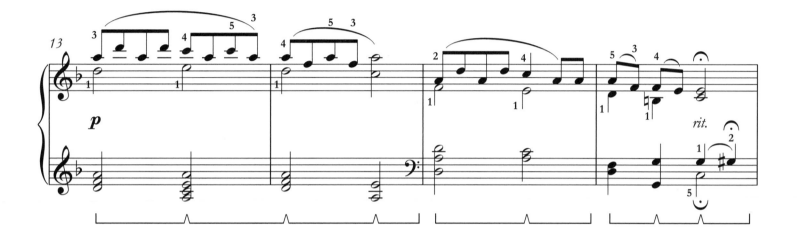

Romeo and Juliet

(Overture)

Pyotr Ilyich Tchaikovsky
1840–1893

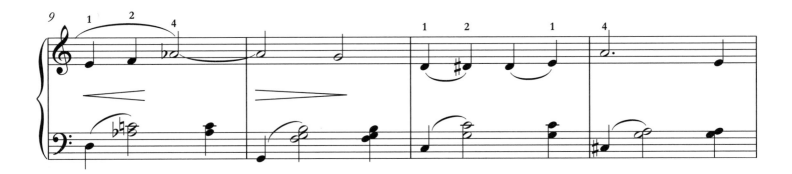

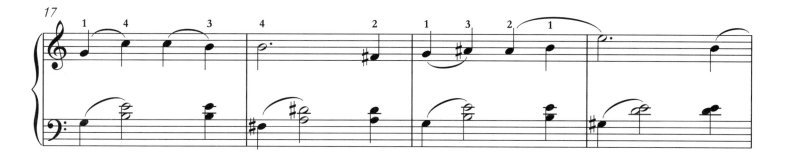

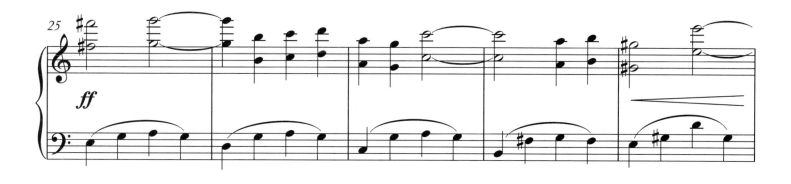

Concerto No. 2

(3rd Movement Theme)

Sergei Rachmaninoff
1873–1943

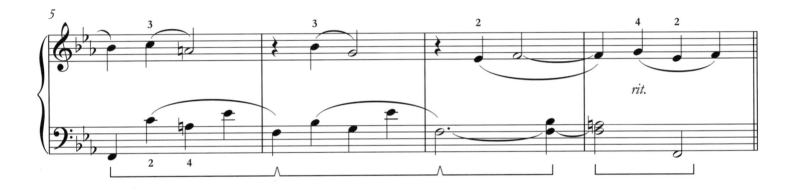

This excerpt from the third movement of Rachmaninoff's second piano concerto could have been more easily notated in B-flat Major. However, C Minor is the key used in the concerto.

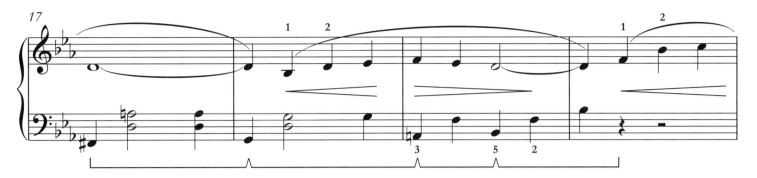

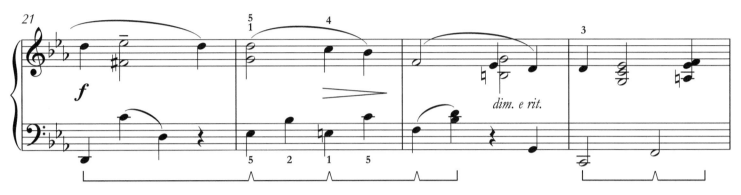

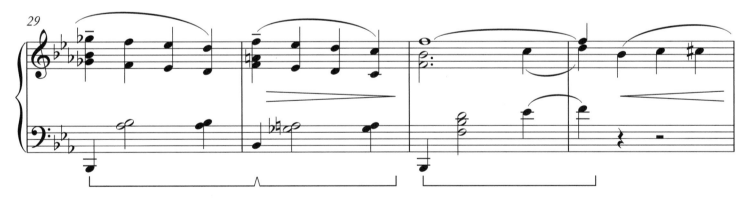

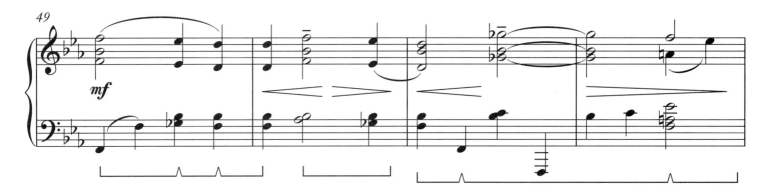

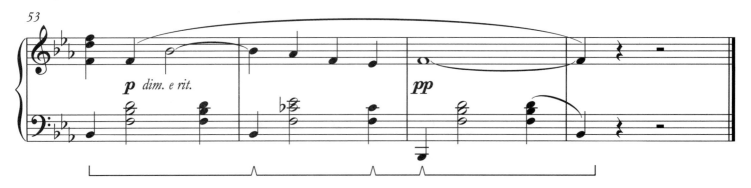

Humoresque
(Op. 101, No. 7)

Antonín Dvořák
1841–1904

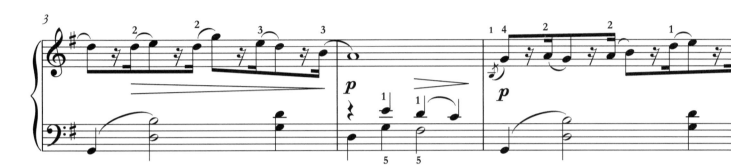

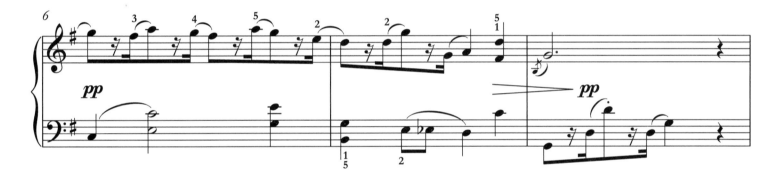

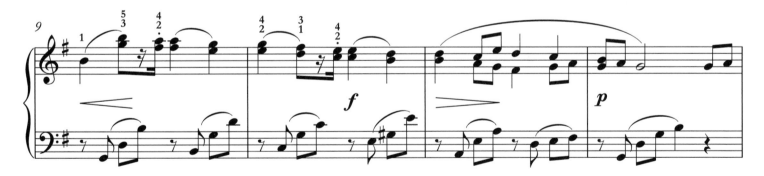

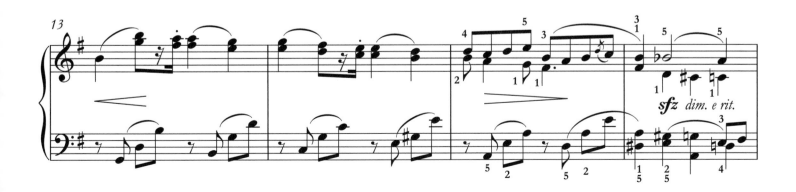

84

Tempo I

(pedal lightly)

The Rosary

Ethelbert Nevin
1862–1901

Andante moderato (♩ = 80)

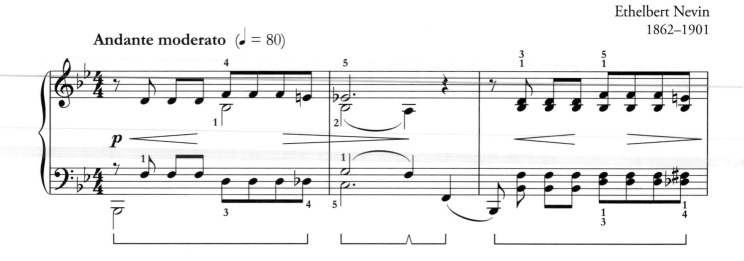

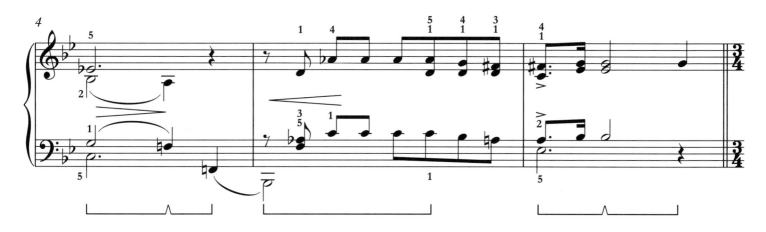

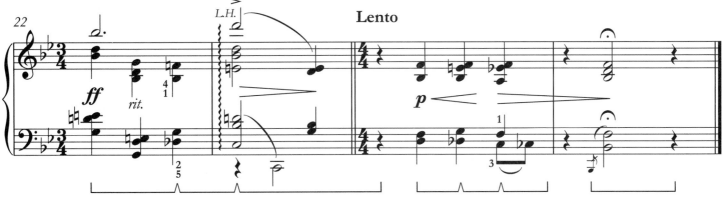

SCALE FINGERING

| SCALES BEGINNING ON WHITE KEYS | SCALES BEGINNING ON BLACK KEYS |

MAJOR SCALES

Right Hand

The thumb falls on the 1st and 4th notes of the scale.

Left Hand

The thumb falls on the 1st and 5th notes of the scale.

HINT:

3rd FINGERS OF BOTH HANDS ALWAYS PLAY TOGETHER.

There are two exceptions to the above rules—the scales of B Major and F Major.

B MAJOR—*Begin with 4th finger in the LH.* Thumbs of both hands always play together.

F MAJOR—*End with 4th finger in the RH.* Thumbs of both hands always play together.

MINOR SCALES

The WHITE KEY MINOR scales are fingered exactly the same as the WHITE KEY MAJOR scales.

MAJOR SCALES

Right Hand

4th finger on B♭ (or A♯).

Left Hand

4th finger on the 4th note of the scale.
Begin with 3rd finger.

There is one exception to the above rules—the G♭ Major scale (or F♯). For this scale use the *Rule of Twos and Threes*, i.e. where TWO BLACK KEYS lie together, use the fingers 2 and 3. Where THREE BLACK KEYS lie together, use the fingers 2, 3 and 4.

MINOR SCALES

B♭ MINOR }
E♭ MINOR } Use the *Rule of Twos and Threes* in BOTH hands.

A♭ (or G♯) MINOR—Fingered same as MAJOR.

D♭ (or C♯) MINOR ⎫

Right Hand

4th finger on the 2nd note of scale.

Left Hand

G♭ (or F♯) MINOR ⎭ *Rule of Twos and Threes*

THE THREE MINOR FORMS

SHOWING THE EVOLUTION OF THE MINOR SCALE

C MAJOR SCALE

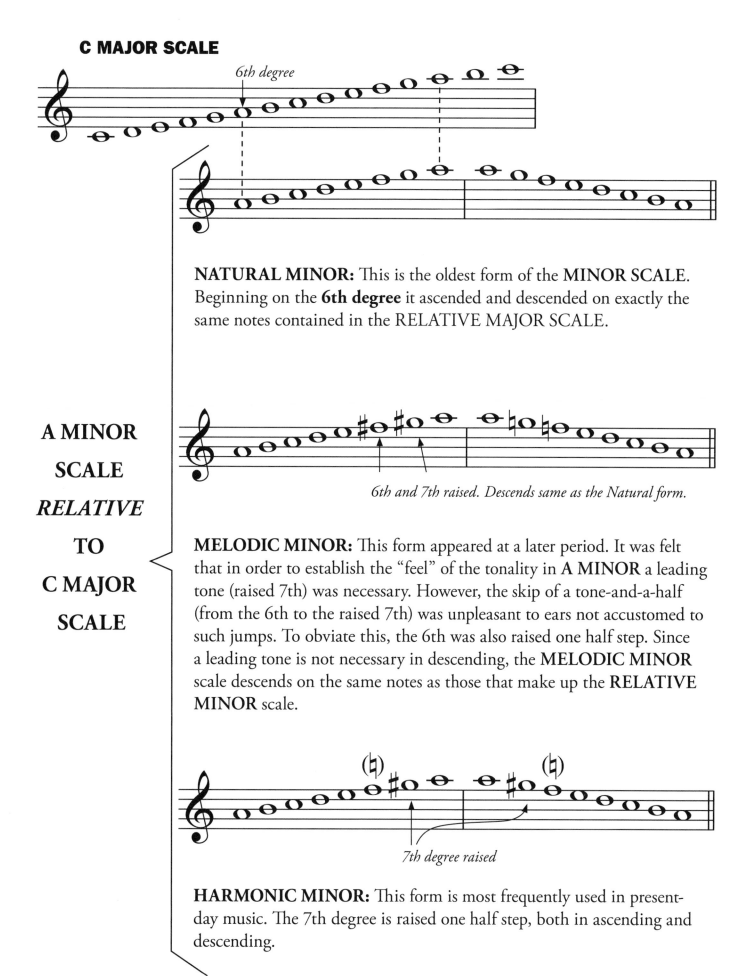

NATURAL MINOR: This is the oldest form of the **MINOR SCALE**. Beginning on the **6th degree** it ascended and descended on exactly the same notes contained in the RELATIVE MAJOR SCALE.

6th and 7th raised. Descends same as the Natural form.

A MINOR SCALE *RELATIVE* TO C MAJOR SCALE

MELODIC MINOR: This form appeared at a later period. It was felt that in order to establish the "feel" of the tonality in **A MINOR** a leading tone (raised 7th) was necessary. However, the skip of a tone-and-a-half (from the 6th to the raised 7th) was unpleasant to ears not accustomed to such jumps. To obviate this, the 6th was also raised one half step. Since a leading tone is not necessary in descending, the **MELODIC MINOR** scale descends on the same notes as those that make up the **RELATIVE MINOR** scale.

7th degree raised

HARMONIC MINOR: This form is most frequently used in present-day music. The 7th degree is raised one half step, both in ascending and descending.

GLOSSARY

Signs or Abbreviations	Terms	Meaning
>	accent	To emphasize or stress a certain note or beat
	allegretto	Light and lively
	allegro	Fast
	andante	Slow
	andantino	Slow—but not as slow as *andante*
	animato	With animation
	arpeggio	In the style of a harp—broken chord
	a tempo	Resume original tempo
⊲	crescendo	A gradual increase in the tone
D.C.	Da Capo	Return to the beginning
D.C. al Fine	Da Capo al Fine	Return to the beginning and play to *Fine*
D.S. al Fine	Dal Segno al Fine	Return to the 𝄋 and play to *Fine*
⊳	diminuendo	A gradual decrease in the tone
	espressivo	Expressively
Fine	Finale	The end
f	forte	Loud
ff	fortissimo	Very loud
	largo	Very slowly
	legato	Connected, bound together
mf	mezzo forte	Moderately loud
mp	mezzo piano	Moderately soft
	moderato	At a moderate tempo
	molto	Much
	nocturne	Night song
8va⌐ (8vb⌐)	octave above (lower)	Play all notes under this sign one octave higher (lower) than written
⌢	pause, fermata	To hold or pause, according to taste
p	piano	Softly
pp	pianissimo	Very softly
	poco	Little
rit.	ritardando	A gradual slowing of the tempo
♩̄	sostenuto	Sustained—with singing quality
♩̇	staccato	Detached
	tempo	Time—rate of speed
♪♪♪ ³	triplet	Three notes to be played in the time normally given to two

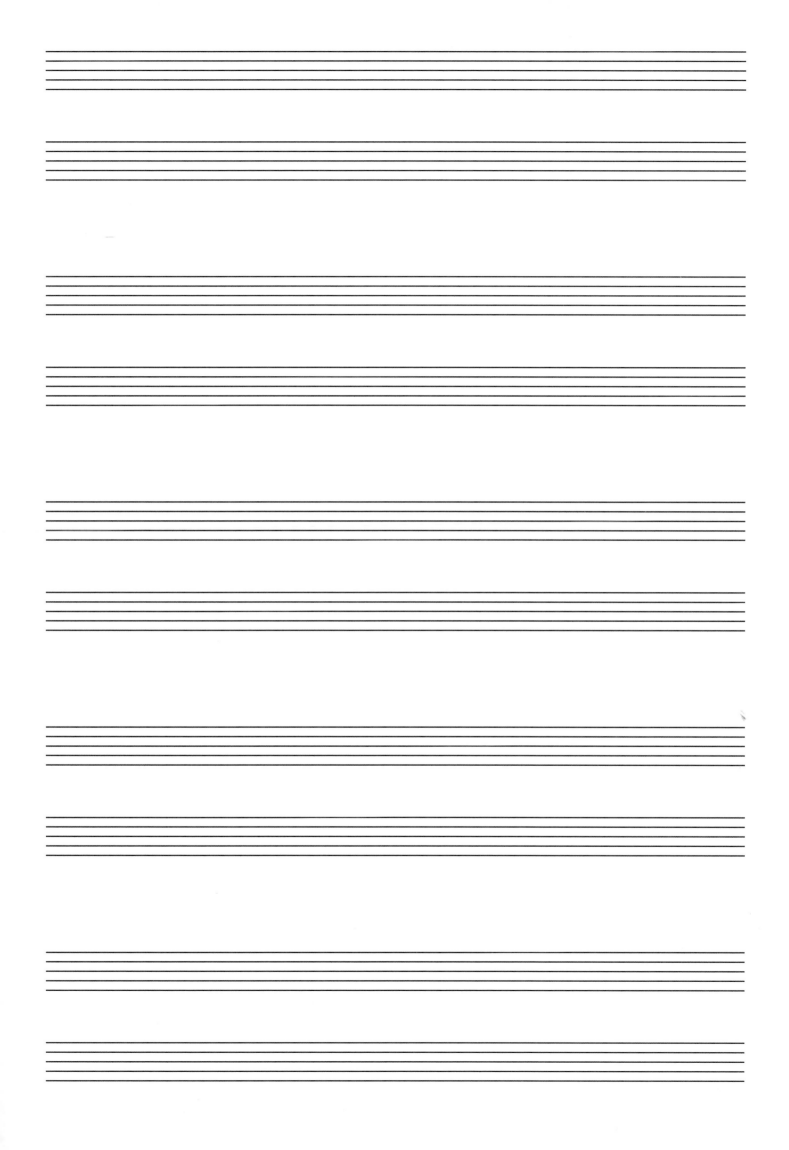

NOTES

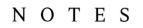

N O T E S

N O T E S

 **John Thompson** (1889-1963) was born in Williamstown, Pennsylvania, the eldest of four children. He began music study at the age of five, and studied piano with Maurits Leefson at the Leefson-Hille Conservatory (Philadelphia), and composition with Dr. Hugh Clark at the University of Pennsylvania. In his early twenties, Thompson toured the United States and Europe as a concert pianist, performing with several prominent European orchestras. Upon his return he began a distinguished career as a pedagogue, heading music conservatories in Indianapolis, Philadelphia, and Kansas City. Today his legacy lies in the continued popularity of his remarkable method books, *Teaching Little Fingers to Play*, *Modern Course*, and *Easiest Piano Course*, used by teachers in the United States and abroad.